Comin' thro' the Rye.
A novel. [By Helen B.
Mathers, afterwards Reeves.]

Anonymous

The BiblioLife Network

This project was made possible in part by the BiblioLife Network (BLN), a project aimed at addressing some of the huge challenges facing book preservationists around the world. The BLN includes libraries, library networks, archives, subject matter experts, online communities and library service providers. We believe every book ever published should be available as a high-quality print reproduction; printed on- demand anywhere in the world. This insures the ongoing accessibility of the content and helps generate sustainable revenue for the libraries and organizations that work to preserve these important materials.

The following book is in the "public domain" and represents an authentic reproduction of the text as printed by the original publisher. While we have attempted to accurately maintain the integrity of the original work, there are sometimes problems with the original book or micro-film from which the books were digitized. This can result in minor errors in reproduction. Possible imperfections include missing and blurred pages, poor pictures, markings and other reproduction issues beyond our control. Because this work is culturally important, we have made it available as part of our commitment to protecting, preserving, and promoting the world's literature.

GUIDE TO FOLD-OUTS, MAPS and OVERSIZED IMAGES

In an online database, page images do not need to conform to the size restrictions found in a printed book. When converting these images back into a printed bound book, the page sizes are standardized in ways that maintain the detail of the original. For large images, such as fold-out maps, the original page image is split into two or more pages.

Guidelines used to determine the split of oversize pages:

• Some images are split vertically; large images require vertical and horizontal splits.
• For horizontal splits, the content is split left to right.
• For vertical splits, the content is split from top to bottom.
• For both vertical and horizontal splits, the image is processed from top left to bottom right.

12636.bb.1

COMIN' THRO' THE RYE.

A Novel.

" Had we never met sae kindly,
  Had we never loved sae blindly,
  Never met and never parted,
  We had ne'er been broken hearted."

IN THREE VOLUMES.

VOL. II.

LONDON:

RICHARD BENTLEY AND SON,

NEW BURLINGTON STREET.

1875.

Caxton Printing Works, Beccles.

SUMMER.

COMIN' THRO' THE RYE.

CHAPTER I.

LEAR. So young and so untender?
CORDELIA. So young, my lord, and true.

I AM eighteen years old. It sounds a good
deal, does it not? It seems only yesterday
that I was quite little, scrambling about in
short frocks and leaving bits of the same on
every railing, hedge, and gate the place contains: now I am in "tails," real downright
tails; limited, it is true, as to length and
width, but still tails which come in useful
when I want to snub Dorley or the
boys; but on the other hand, hamper me
sadly when some forlorn remnant of my
active youth prompts me to scale the trees,
or go bird's-nesting. On the whole I am

sorry to have reached that broad flat table-
land of grown-upness that is so easy to
ascend, but can be stepped down from never
again. If one's young days might only be
pushed farther, if we might be given
thirty years of growing instead of sixteen,
surely the forty beyond, that are allotted
as the period of man's existence, would be
enough for us to be grown-up, and steady,
and sad in? I hate to part with my merry
insouciant young years. I dread to let them
go, and feel the old tastes and loves slipping
away from me, and the new fancies and
pursuits taking their place. I am sorry
that I shall never grow any more—never
measure my back against the school-room
wall to see if my head is any nearer the
notch that marks Jack's height—never look
anxiously in the glass to see if time brings
me less ugliness as she brings more inches
(for at eighteen one is able to form a pretty
tolerable estimate of what one is going to
be like for the rest of one's days)—never go
donkey riding, or pig-nut hunting, or shrimp
getting, any more—never love bulls'-eyes,
blackberries, and treacle tarts with the

exceeding love that I knew for them of yore. I can even get over a gate without feeling any over-mastering impulse to vault or leap it. I can see Pepper taking an ecstatic roll in the grass without straightway longing to cast myself down and roll too. The kitchen-garden has lost some of its charm in my eyes, for, thanks to my being so old, other affairs than gooseberries and currants occupy my mind, very much against my will. I am the eldest daughter at home now, and obliged to mind my morals and manners to a maddening extent; for every sin of omission and commission of my brothers and sisters is laid to my charge, and said to be the fruit of my "example." It is dismal at the Manor House now so many are away. Jack is in London. He is going to be a barrister, and I call it *mean* of him; for if he had only elected to be a fat gentleman farmer, I could have gone and lived with him in a little house, and been as happy—— Well! brothers never love their sisters quite as their sisters love them.

Milly has been "woo'd an' married an' a'"

over a year and a half, and the family has
not done gasping over the miraculous event
yet. How it fell out that papa's unwilling
consent was wrung from him; and how she
never ran away at all, but stood up to be
married, in a white satin gown and trimmings; and how papa gave her away with
an ineffable hitch of his nose; and how up
to the very last moment every one believed
that he did not mean her to be married at
all, but intended to turn the whole affair
into a joke; and how he disappointed us
all, as he always does :—are not these things
writ in the chronicles of the house of Adair?

After so far forgetting himself as to make
two people happy, he gave it to be understood in the family that nothing else of the
kind would be permitted to take place for
another century or so, and that this lapse of
authority on his part was not to be taken
as a precedent, but regarded in the light of
a comet, a plague, or any other irresponsible
appearance for which there is no account-
ing. About two years ago Alice was
formally forgiven, and invited to stay here,
with her little son; but the sight of her

perfect liberty of speech and action, the amplitude of her petticoats, the abundance of her pin-money, were too much for him, and the flag of truce came down with a run. If the governor could put his thoughts into rhyme, I think he would say :—

> "Oh ! while my daughters with me stayed,
> Would I had *whacked* them more !"

It must be hard to know that they have got safely out of his clutches; and that he may have nothing in the future to reproach himself with on my account, he makes my existence an uncommonly pleasant thing. Sometimes I feel that I must run away, or that it would be better to marry anything than live the life I lead. Common sense, however, whispers that a spinster's troubles are but passing ones; but, once married, she must sit down under her misfortunes, and bear them to her life's end. For married folks have their troubles, have they not? just like single ones. Oh! what a black bitter hour that must be, when a woman lifts her eyes, and looking at her husband, sitting opposite her, realizes for the first time that she has made *a mistake!* "Men," says Madame Scudéri, "should keep their eyes wide open before marriage, and half shut after." Surely women may very safely say the same?

I wonder why I have fallen on the subject of matrimony this afternoon? I am wandering alone through the garden, bright with its late July pomp of geraniums and verbenas, and across the orchard into the wide hot fields. There is no shade anywhere, but my big sun-bonnet is tipped over my nose, so I may defy sunstroke; and in "my mind's hi," as I once heard a man, of more worth than letters, remark, I see a cool, shady, green little chamber, of which the ceiling is woven branches, and the carpet of mossy grass, while the walls are made of the sturdy brown bodies of the oak and the beech. It is not far away, but it is shut in so deftly that a stranger might pass it by close and never see it, though he went through the field of rye that stretches out to its left in a whitely ruffled sea of light. "After all," I say to myself, as I turn out of the last big field into a cool, shady alley through which a brook runs, "what does it matter if the governor *is* troublesome? He can't take away any of God's gifts from us; and all the tempers and hard words in creation could not take the glow out of this summer afternoon, or the colour out of the sky, no, never!"

Thus moralizing, I sit down by the brook to rest for a moment before sallying forth into the sun-flooded fields of grain; and it seems to answer "Never!" as it hurries along over the clear stones, not knowing when it is well off, sighing to lose itself in the wide river. Its babble sounds very pretty, as though it were talking to the fragrant meadowsweet that borders its banks like foam, or the yellow milfoil that Jack and I call ladies'-slippers—a frivolous substitute for the grand old name of lotus, of which there are three species, and this common unbeautiful yellow is one. Lotus! what an exquisite name it is! and what exquisite visions it brings up before us! The river is a rare sun-worshipper: almost all his flowers are either yellow or gold-coloured: look at those brazen marigolds yonder, and those handsome irises a yard away: and

farther down, where he deepens into a
mimic lake, lie more yellow flowers, great
sleepy, languid lilies, to do him honour and
deck his breast. It is a relief to look away
at the forget-me-nots, with their innocent
candid eyes, that look straight into mine,
saying as plain as they can speak, "Do
not forget me!"

A bee-orchis lifts itself out of the hedge,
straight and tall, with its absurd resemblance to the insect, as though it had
alighted freshly on the flower, and been
frozen there, retaining its exquisite colours.
The hollyhocks, "emblem of cruelty and
pride," stand stiff and stately. I wonder
if ever at night their speckled bells ring
out a dainty peal of music learned in
Hollyhock land? The reed-mace stand
round, tall and bare: with their long
stalks and olive-brown spikes, they look too
obstinate to shiver and shake; yet a curse
lies upon them—for was not one of their
number placed in the Victim's hand in direst
mockery as a sceptre? Yonder, in the pale
blue blossoms of the ivy-leaved bell-flower,
lies a naughty, sleepy little insect which

Linnæus named Florissimus, from its love of sleeping in flowers. He must be a luxurious dainty little Sybarite and a happy, to be able to choose his couch of red, white, pink, or blue, at will; while we, poor mortals, have to seek our dull four-posters night after night.

I pick up my sun-bonnet, put it on, and lean over the stile that lies between me and the corn-field, that is turning brighter and more golden day by day under the sun's fierce beams. The scarlet poppy-heads, gorgeous vagrants, with their leaves as freshly crinkled as though they had but just left Nature's laundry, nod imperiously at me, saying, "Gather me! gather me!" The corn-cockle, pride of the harvest-field, and abomination of the farmer, cries "I am handsomest, pick *me!*" The field knautia lifts her insolent head high above the corn, seeming to say, "See how much higher a parasite can climb than her master!" The pheasant's-eye, or the flower of Adonis (over which, as the story runs, the life blood of Adonis gushed, staining its white petals crimson) looks up invitingly; the pansies, "three faces under one hood," as the country folk call them, from their lowly seat at the roots of the corn, please the eye with their modest velvet-eyed beauty. And, since I know and love them every one, I dash in amongst the corn and gather my hands full. A scentless, bright-hued, vagabond cluster they make; for they are but saucy parasites, that love to creep about and hamper the knees of the strong, beneficent grain, as all useless gaudy things ever do about the stalwart and brave. Already the scarlet pimpernel—the only wild flower that dares dispute the poppy's pre-eminence in colour, has closed its leaves, for it is past three o'clock. I wonder how it always knows the time so exactly, when human people's watches are so often out of gear? The intolerable heat stops my somewhat unreasonable speculations, so I hastily retreat to the brook, and there weave my flowers into a garland, with many a nodding grass and leaf between, idly, carelessly, for no other reason than that my hands are idle and the flowers are pretty playthings.

When I have finished it I turn it round
and round and marvel whether Ophelia's
could by any possibility have looked any
madder? Poor lost Ophelia!

> " Larded all with sweet flowers
>   Which bewept to the grave did go,
>   With true-love showers."

Whose drowned face comes to us so freshly
across the dead centuries, while the echo
of her sweet voice singing, "Lord, we know
what we are; but we-know not what we
may be," lives in our hearts with all our
household words and treasures. I always
think of Ophelia as a slender maiden, with
far-away dreamy grey eyes, that saw Death
beckoning to her, in strange and lovely
guise, down among the rushes, and to
whom she went gaily decked with flowers,
as a bride to her bridegroom. I wonder
if Ophelia had long hair, and whether it was
golden, or yellow, or brown like mine? It
ought to have been yellow—every woman
should be fair, every man should be dark,
in my opinion. I don't think many young
women could drown themselves with
decency now-a-days: their locks are not

ample enough, unless eked out with pilfer-
ings from the impecunious living and
helpless dead. And if they tied any
false curls and tails on for the occasion,
it would somewhat take the edge off our
pity to see the hapless maiden lying in
one place, and her back hair in another.
We Adairs are well off in the respect of
head coverings, rather too well off in fact;
for in hot weather our abundant manes
are no joke, and we are inclined to envy
our more lightly crowned neighbours who
appear at church in chignons, that are the
most innocent of deceptions, and provoke
mirth, not admiration. Only last Sunday
a disastrous casualty occurred to a farmer's
wife sitting in the pew exactly before us.
Her chignon parted its moorings, and, sus-
pended by a single wisp, hung down her
back and over our pew, bobbing up and
down in a horribly active manner, causing
lively fear in our ranks; for in the too
probable event of its falling into our midst,
who among us would be found to possess
sufficient *aplomb* to hand it to the denuded
lady?

I pull off my sun-bonnet, for no one is likely to see me, and the cows yonder will tell no tales; and putting my wreath upon my head bend over the brook to try and see my own reflection. Close to the edge there is a little shallow, fenced about with sticks and stones, and in it I see my face, framed in its poppy wreath and loose veil of brown hair.

"Not bad!" I say aloud. "Now if your nose were a little longer, and your mouth a little smaller, you wouldn't be an ill-looking young person, as girls go; but as it is, you are precisely what your amiable papa says— you are the—— "

"Prettiest little girl in Christendom," says a man's voice behind me, making me start so violently that I nearly topple over into the brook.

"Did I not tell you," I say, without turning my head, "that I was tired to death of the very sight of you; and that you were not to come near me for three whole days?"

"The three whole days will be up to-morrow, Nell."

"To-morrow is not to-day," I say, turning round. "Now I wonder what you would say if you were followed everywhere by a tiresome, teazing shadow, that never left you alone for a single moment, and the more you told it to go away the more it stopped?"

"Everybody has a shadow," he says, "I among the rest."

"Does your shadow make love to you?" I ask, stamping my foot on the soft grass. "Whether you will or no, does it?"

"No, it does not," he says shortly. "Go on, Nell; don't be afraid of hurting my feelings!"

"Then you should not worry me so. Now I have had quite a little holiday the last two days, and of course you have come this afternoon to spoil it all! If you would only talk to me sensibly, as Jack does—— "

"Only I am not Jack," he says—"worse luck. You would like me if I were."

"I like you now," I say quickly; "next to mother and the rest of them, I do not know any one I like so well. Why can't you be satisfied with that?"

"Nell," says the young man, standing before me, straight and tall and fair in the sunlight, with a vexed look in his blue eyes, and restless fingers that tug at his yellow moustache, "what did you promise me four years ago?"

"That when I was eighteen and six months old I would marry you, if I had not seen any one I liked better."

"And you are going to break your promise?"

"No," I say, looking up into his honest face. "Did I not tell you once that I never broke my promises? But you must give me time, George; you must not hurry me. I am not very old yet, you know; and love isn't easy to learn all at once. I wouldn't promise you anything I did not mean to stick to; but if I said to-day that I loved you, and would marry you, it would be wrong, for I do not think I am the least in the world in love with you, do you?"

"No," he says, with a rueful sigh, "there can't be very much doubt on that score!"

"So," I say with alacrity, "I will wait till I am in love with you before we settle it all. Don't you think it would be much pleasanter?"

"For you, perhaps," he says, "but I know my own heart."

"Do you know," I say diffidently, "that sometimes I think you don't go the right way to work to make me love you? If you were to be cross sometimes, or—or shake me—or something—I don't exactly know what. Perhaps if you made me jealous now, for a girl hates any one else to have her lover, even if she does not want him herself, you know——"

I pause. After all it is not easy to instruct a young man how to woo you; but I am so really anxious to fall in love with George, and so sorry for him, that I would take any pains to cultivate the gentle passion.

"I don't think you meant that," says George, with as much scorn as his manly, pleasant voice will borrow; "or if you did, I can't follow you. I know there are women who don't care a rap for a man as long as he is entirely their own, but directly he turns up his nose at them they are head over heels in love with him; but I never thought you were one of that sort, Nell. Now, when a man loves a girl he doesn't like her any the better, I can tell you, for staring at and hankering after this man and that. All her value is gone in his eyes if she does not stick to him in thought, word, and deed. Her flirtations with any one else provoke disgust, not love; and she makes him feel not so much piqued as *small*."

"And that a man hates to look," I say slyly. "Touch any man's or woman's self-conceit, and they never forgive you!"

"It is not self-conceit," he says stoutly; "it is self-respect."

"I wish you were not so honest a man," I say, looking at him wistfully; "perhaps if you were not so good I should like you better."

I wonder what it is that George lacks, and which holds me back from acknowledging him lover and master? He is the best bred, best mannered, best grown man I ever saw; he is likable, true, admirable in every way; and if he does not find favour in my eyes, it is hard to say who will. And yet I feel that I could love—ay, and well too, when the right man came, but I may never meet my Prince Charming, and as years go by dawdle into a comfortable, safe, friendly affection for my yellow-haired lover yonder. Perhaps if we had begun with "a little aversion" it might have been more hopeful, our exchange of words would have been heartier, brisker. In squabbles there is some heat, and I always think the people who quarrel the most fiercely love each other best; they must have power to move each other or they would not bandy so many useless words.

Long ago I took off my poppy wreath, and now I am swinging it slowly backwards and forwards.

"George," I say, looking at him thoughtfully, "were you ever very wicked?"

"Why?"

"Nothing," I say; "only to be wicked gives experience. I have heard experience is nice, is it not?"

"That depends on the sort a man gets."

"Did any one ever jilt you?" I ask. "Have you ever made love to any one before me?"

The young man looks at me with a queer kind of half shame on his face.

"And if I had," he asks, "would you mind?"

"I should be delighted!" I say quickly. "If you had made love to people, and been thrown overboard, you know, and people had made love to you, you would be so much better qualified to make love to me! I should like to have a lover who had been in love hundreds of times, but considered me the nicest and liked me the best of all! That would be something to be proud of, would it not?"

"You don't understand about these things, dear," he says sadly. "If you cared for me you would wish to be the first girl I had ever loved. You would begrudge those other women having known me before you did."

"I wonder what it is to care," I say, drawing a long tress of hair through my fingers, and looking down at the water flowing at our feet. "If to care for you is to like you very much when you are not making love to me, then I care for you very much indeed!"

But George does not answer; he is looking straight away over my head at the distant hills, thinking hard and deep, and the misery in his blue eyes hurts me. I never could bear to see anything, even a worm, suffer.

"George," I say, slipping my hand into his, "don't fret about it; perhaps it will come in time, you know, and——"

"Have you ever seen the man you *could* care about?" he asks, stroking my hand gently between his own.

"In my dreams, perhaps," I say laughing. "Where else could I have met him?"

"You have never been away from home," he goes on, "save to school; and you could not see any one there. But do you know, Nell, sometimes I have thought that the reason you don't love me is because you have a fancy for somebody else? A silly notion, is it not?"

"Very!" I say, taking my hand away. "Did you suspect me of an unlawful love of Skippy?"

"God forbid!" he says, laughing. "No! I did not suspect you of that misplaced tenderness! Do you know, Nell, that I think you are the coldest little thing I ever saw! I don't believe any one would ever move you."

"I am not tender," I say, making a grimace; "none of us are—we all had that nonsense knocked out of us in our youth; but I am true!"

"Are you?" he cries eagerly. "Then when these six months are up——"

"I shall keep my promise," I say, my heart sinking; "only (reviving) don't make too sure of me, for six months is a long time, and there is no knowing whom I may see in it!"

"I am not afraid," says George, smiling. How happy he looks! "No one ever comes to Silverbridge, and you never go away, so how can any one see you."

"Don't forget," I say, by way of damping his exhilaration, "that papa will have to be asked."

And for the first time in my life, my parents' little prejudices on the subject of marriage commend themselves favourably to my eyes.

"That doesn't matter," says George. "Mrs. Lovelace ran away!"

"But there were exceptional circumstances in that case," I say with dignity. "Besides, it would never do for that sort of thing to become a habit in the family. They were properly engaged for a long while!"

"And why may not you and I be?"

"Because he would never hear of it!" I say, looking forward with dismay to that dreadful engaged period of "pecking" that I have until now successfully evaded.

"Your governor and mine get on splendidly," says George, in a hopeful voice. "That would surely go for something?"

"That is one of those things no one can understand," I say, shaking my head. "My father has known your father for four years, and they have not quarrelled yet! Mr. Tempest must have the temper of an angel, or papa has never kicked him, because he thought he was so little, and old, and frail!"

"Which redounds to Colonel Adair's credit," says George, laughing; "but I have often wondered he does not take a turn at me!"

"Don't be afraid," I say, nodding. "As soon as he knows you are anxious to have him for a father-in-law, he will be good for any amount of that. Is it not droll that parents should see things going on under their very noses, and then be so surprised and disgusted when anything comes of it?"

"I suppose their fathers were before them?" says George; "and some day we shall be the same! I say, Nell, what a little duck you look, to be sure!" he says, as after stooping over the water, I turn round with my wreath set jauntily on my head.

"You have not half admired me yet!" I say, holding out my dress; "nor do you know what I am going to do?"

"Stay with me."

"I am going to walk across the field of corn, and then the field of rye, just as I am, and then——"

"Well, and then?"

"——I am going to sit down," I say guardedly. Not for worlds would I have

George know of my little green parlour. He would spend half his days in it!

"And I shall come with you," he says promptly, "in case you meet anybody with that wreath on your head."

"No, you will not," I say decidedly. "What good would you be to me, pray? and who am I likely to meet, except a plough-man, whose looks I should mind about as much as the stare of that cow yonder? I am going by myself."

"Very well," he says, sitting down on the stile, "I will wait here until you come back!"

Now, if there be anything harassing, it is to know that some one is waiting for you round the corner, and counting the minutes to your arrival. To enjoy one's self is impossible—some of his discomfort is passed on to you, and the result is nasty.

"I always thought," I say with dignity, "that when a person was not wanted, he generally *went*."

"Thank you!" says George, jumping up with alacrity. "I won't require you to say that *twice*.'

And away he stalks, his head well up, while I take the seat he has just left vacant and congratulate myself on the success of that last shot. Really I never saw him go away so quickly before! What a nice back he has! How well he walks! he ought to have been a soldier! He is really cross this time, for he does not turn his head once.

And now for a rush across that burning, broiling, expanse of grain. I fly along so fast, my feet scarcely touch the ground, and as I go I sing a verse of the old, old song—

> "Gin a body meet a body, comin' thro' the rye,
> And a body kiss a body, need a body cry?"

I never could sing a bit, but there is no one by to hear me, and I feel so unaccountably joyously happy, as though I *must* make a noise. With my head bent to avoid the level glare of the sun, I see nothing approaching me, and butt head foremost into a black something. . . . "I beg your pardon!" I say, as I hastily recoil, and put up my hand to tear off my ridiculous wreath. "I beg your pardon!" And then lift my eyes and see that this *something* is

Paul Vasher. And I stand staring at him with my poppy wreath in my hand, mute as a stock fish—I who have the longest, glibbest tongue in christendom—with never a word to say for myself. Although I know him, he does not know me. There is no recognition in his glance, only an alert sort of surprise; but, thank Heaven, no amusement, which is under the circumstances simply angelic in him. My heart is crying over and over again, "He has come back! He has come back!" with a glad, breathless hurry that amazes me; but my lips are dumb, my hand does not steal out in friendly greeting, and if ever a young woman looked an awkward, gaping, silly bit of rusticity, that young woman is me. For the first time in all my life, perhaps, I do not take the first word, and he speaks.

"I am trying to find my way to the Manor House, but I am not sure if I am in the right path. Can you direct me?"

His voice breaks the spell, my tongue begins to wag again.

"I am going that way, and will show you."

I turn my back upon him, for the path is narrow, wondering heartily whether he is relieving his feelings by having a good grin at my back? Such a figure as I look! though on the whole I fancy my back view is not quite as disreputable as my front. Shall I turn and ascertain? No, for it is always more bearable to suspect people are making fun of you than to *know* it. Arrived at the stile I find myself in a dilemma: to scramble over it anyhow by myself is one thing, to be delicately assisted over it by a gentleman another; for it consists of a single upright slab of stone that affords no foothold whatever, and the only legitimate means of surmounting it is to take it in your stride or vault it. In the present instance I can do neither, so I look in sore perplexity from Mr. Vasher to the stile, and from the stile to him, until, he probably seeing the difficulty, we catch each other's eye and go off into sudden laughter.

"I never saw anything in the least like that before," he says. "Was it erected for acrobats?"

"I think so!" I say, recovering. "But

please do not attempt to help me over, or we shall infallibly roll into the brook! Now, if you would not mind walking on and turning your back I can manage it quite well by myself!" He walks on, for he is a man of sense—a fool would stand on the other side of the stile and argue the matter for half an hour—and I am over it, and after him like a shot.

"Do you know," he says, as I join him, "that when I saw you come dancing towards me I could not believe you were mortal? I thought (laughing) that you must be the goddess of joy dropped out of a cloud, you looked so happy."

"And may not one be happy?" I ask, looking at him in surprise. "Are not all folks sometimes?"

"Sometimes," he says; "but moderately, not so overflowingly as you were."

"Ah! if you only knew all my troubles," I say, shaking my head, "you would wonder I could ever laugh at all! And yet I do, morning, noon, and night. I often think I shall be punished some day for having such a light heart."

"Fuller says, 'An ounce of contentment is worth a pound of sadness to serve God with,' so I don't think you will be heavily judged!"

"By the by," I say, turning very red and dropping my voice, "when you met me just now you did not hear me *singing*, did you?"

"Of course! Why?"

"And you did not laugh?"

"There was nothing to laugh at!"

"I will tell you a secret," I say smiling. (May I not be confidential with him, since I knew him so many years ago, when I was quite little and childish?) "I would give the world to be able to sing, but I never could. It seems so natural to sing when one is happy, does it not? Just as a bird breaks out into song, because he feels that life is good and he loves it. I had singing lessons at Pimpernel once, and the man did his very best with me, but at last he gave it up. One must be bad, must one not, before a singing master washes his hands of you? About two years ago Milly (my sister, you know) and I were at a little party at the

Vicarage, and I stood up to sing a duet with her. It was a foolhardy thing to do, but I had practised it for weeks; and when I opened my mouth there was not a sound to be heard—literally not a sound. Perhaps it was as well—but oh! I was so bitterly ashamed. I think I sat down and turned my face to the wall and wept."

"And did your sister sing it alone?" asks Mr. Vasher, laughing.

"She sang another instead!"

"It is very odd," says Paul, "but I know your voice quite well—I am sure I have heard it before; and your face seems familiar to me."

"People are so alike," I say evasively, turning my head away from his keen regard. Somehow I do not want him to recollect me just yet. "Nature makes all her people in sets, and mine is a common pattern."

"I think not," he says slowly; "for I never saw but one person a bit like you before, and that was Helen Adair."

I see his mind trembling on the brink of a discovery, so I hastily hold up my poppy wreath for his inspection.

"Look!" I say, "is it not *bizarre*, extraordinary? Did not that make you smile?"

He takes it from my hand and turns it round. "It looked very pretty on," he says. "Did you make it yourself, Nell?"

"You know who I am: you knew it all along!" I say, starting back.

"Only since a moment ago," he says smiling. "And now, after all these years, have you not a welcome for me?"

I hold out both my hands with a deep sigh. "If you only knew how glad I am you have come back!" I say—"how I have wished for you to come back! You have been away four whole years."

"And you remembered me all that while?" he says, looking down into my face eagerly—"you missed me?"

"So much," I say gravely, "that often I have said to Jack, that if I knew where you were I should write and ask you if you had forgotten your promise about the fruit garden."

"And that was the only reason you wanted to see me back?"

"Oh no! I wanted to see you too."

He seems to have forgotten he is holding my hands, so I take them away.

"Are you married?" I ask, looking up at the dark strong face, that is altered no whit, save that the restless expression has fallen away from it, and a better, nobler look grown upon it.

"No."

"I am so glad," I say, clapping my hands; "so glad! Do not be angry with me, but after you went away I used always to think that when I saw you next you would be married to——"

I stop short, I had forgotten he does not know that I know that he loved Silvia Fleming; my cheeks turn scarlet as my poppies at my stupidity.

"Yes," he says, "and to whom?"

"No one in particular," I say, looking down at the grass; "it was only a ridiculous fancy of mine."

We walk on again, and there is a little pause in our brisk conversation; perhaps he is *remembering*, and I am recalling Silvia Fleming's vow, and marvelling if she has tried to win him again, or forgotten her wild love in sober, respectable marriage.

"It was lucky I came through these fields," says Mr. Vasher, "for I was going to the Manor House to see *you*."

"If you want to find me of afternoons," I say, laughing, "you must scour the country and look under every hedge and tree; I live out of doors in the summer. And were you coming to see me so soon? That was good of you."

"Will you believe," he says, looking down on me (my head barely reaches his shoulder, and yet I am a very decent height, five feet four inches), "that you were the first person I thought of when I came back to England? I only arrived at The Towers yesterday, and, as you see, have set out to see you to-day. And, after all, you are a disappointment," he says, with a queer smile. "Somehow I always thought of finding you a bright, frank-faced, honest little girl, just as I left you, and now——" (he scans me slowly from head to foot) "I find you grown up and——"

"I wish you had come back sooner," I

say, interrupting, " for, do you know, I am getting beyond gooseberries, and can exist without apples ! "

We are passing through the orchard now, and several of the fry are standing about in the distance, distinctly marvelling who on earth sister Nell has got hold of. In the garden we meet the governor, and, to my amazement, instead of Mr. Vasher being ignominiously ordered off the premises, papa welcomes him with much politeness, speaks with respect of Mr. Vasher's defunct father, and finally floats him away in a stream of amicable conversation. Verily, this is a world of change !

CHAPTER II.

"There is no woman's sides
Can bide the beating of so strong a passion
As love doth give my heart : no woman's heart
So big to hold so much. . . ."

IT is nearly a month since Mr. Vasher paid his flying visit to Silverbridge, and we are drawing very near that illustrious First, which is the one day of the year to all Englishmen, from the keen sportsman and crack shot to the aimless booby who never goes out with a gun save at the risk of his own and his neighbours' lives. Although the partridges on the Vasher estate may be supposed to have long ago taken to eating each other, as there is no one, save poachers, to shoot them, their owner will not be here to sally forth with his friends, and send them to kingdom come; on the contrary, he is bound over to appear in

S——shire at that date, and will not be among his own stubble until the second week of the month. After that he is going to settle down in his own house, and become, he says, a respectable country gentleman. I wonder why the words "country gentleman" always bring up a vision of a red-faced, fox-hunting, ample-bodied, mutton-chop-whiskered, rather vulgar-looking man, who loves beer and doubtful jokes, and has a weakness for kissing the pretty Maries at roadside inns?

He seemed very sorry to go away, Paul Vasher. Papa says he was absolutely obliged to go, business affairs accumulated, etc., etc. He made a pleasant change; I hope he will come back soon! At the present moment I am walking along the passage that leads to mother's room, with a fresh nosegay of flowers in my hand, for her table.

"Come in!" she says, as I knock; and entering, I find her sitting by the open window, smoothing the primrose-coloured locks of her youngest born with a brush as soft as swan's-down.

I have never written very much about mother, but she is as much the life of her children as the air they breathe; whoever or whatever we love we always place them "after mother." As I give her a hearty hug, I become aware of a pleased smile on her face, that not only lurks in every pretty corner, but covers it as with a garment in a most unequivocal manner.

"*Jack*," I say, with a sudden leap of joy through my veins, "he is coming home?"

"No," says mother, "it is not Jack. It is an invitation."

"An invitation!" I repeat. "Are any of our neighbours mad enough, or forgiving enough, to try that on again?"

"It is from Milly. She wants you to go on the 30th to stay with her for a month."

"Lovely!" I say, with a deep gasp; "but he will not let me go."

"It is just possible that he may," says mother, "although he has refused all Alice's invitations for you. You would like it, dear?"

"Like it," I say, sighing; "did not the country mouse love to go and stay with the

town one, even though he came to terrible
grief? But, mother, mother, I have no
clothes. Running wild here is one thing,
but footing it at Luttrell another."

"What have you got?" asks mother,
setting down her darling, who speedily ac-
complishes his one object in life, which is to
overturn himself.

"One black silk, which is skimpy and
rusty, and tight and green; two decent
white dresses, and one indecent one; a
few prints that look passable enough in
the dim vista of a woodland, but are not
quite, ahem! the thing for visiting. Have
you got anything at all left in the wardrobe?"

Mother's wardrobe is a kind of museum
of dead and gone fashions and garments,
among which she always rummages when
any of us are particularly ragged or naked.
Unfortunately the rummaging of twenty
years has left it very bald and miserable
indeed; and as everything of any value has
been taken out long ago, I stand but a poor
chance of fishing up a garment fit to go
visiting in.

" There is the yellow satin," says mother, " but then you don't like yellow satin."

" Especially when my great grandmother upset a dish of gravy down its front," I say grimacing. " Would you have me like the serving man in 'L'Avare,' who was bidden by his master to hold his hat over his clothes, that the company might not see the rents and stains ? "

"And there is the plum-coloured paduasoy," says mother, unheeding my flippant interjections, " and you don't like that."

" No, I do not! If I can't have one or two moderately respectable gowns I must stay at home."

" I don't know what your papa will say," says mother with a sigh.

" If he only says 'Yes,'" I say, kissing her, " I'll forgive all the rest. Is that other letter from Dolly ? "

" Yes, she likes it very much at Charteris, but she seems rather home-sick."

" Poor Dolly!" I say, " I wish she were back again. I do miss her so. Mother, mother, why did you not have more girls ? "

"Nell," says the Bull of Basan, rushing
in, "the governor says you're to go down
directly; the Tempests are in the garden."

"Bother," I say, crossly; for would I not
a hundred times rather be up here talking
of new gowns with mother, than trotting
round the hot garden and fields with
George, talking of love? I know those
little morning walks round the estate well
enough; and as to the Mummy's being an
invalid, I don't believe a word of it; his
legs are made of cast iron. I follow my
sturdy young brother, who has earned his
nickname by the extraordinary power and
volume of his bellow (when papa is out of
the way), downstairs very unwillingly.

The gentlemen are all standing together
in the porch, and I say "How do you do?"
to the father, and lay my fingers in the
warm grasp of the son; and after that little
formula we all stroll forth together, the two
old souls in front, and we young ones
behind.

"Do you know," I say, lowering my voice
cautiously, for in our family we all firmly
believe that papa has not only eyes but ears

in the back of his head, " that perhaps
something most delightful is going to
happen to me? There is a chance of my
going away? "

"Going away," he repeats blankly, and a
pale dashed look comes over his face; " do
you mean it, Nell?"

"Why should I not?" I ask in astonishment, tipping my sun-bonnet a little farther
forward; "is there anything so very as-
tonishing in that, pray?"

"It would not be in some people, but it
is in you; I thought you never went away."

"That is just why I am so anxious to
begin," I say briskly. "Do you think he
will let me go? do you *think* he will?"

"I don't know," says George, switching
at the grass with his stick; "do you want
to go so very much?"

"I think I should break my heart if I
did not!" I say with conviction. "You see
I have never been anywhere really; and
think of what it would be to go to, perhaps,
a ball (Do you think they will dance at
Luttrell?), and have a real ball dress, and
a real——"

"Lover!" puts in George, with a pale smile; "for you are as sure to have the one as the other!"

"You silly boy!" I say, patting his coat sleeve, "have you not got over that ridiculous notion yet? I wish you were coming too; yes I do, with all my heart!"

"Are you sure of that," he asks, looking into my eyes with those blue ones that have never met mine yet without their warm love-light burning steadily.

"Quite sure!" I say, smitten with a quick compunction; for am I not devoutly glad at the prospect of going away from him? and when did he ever leave me without regret? "You ought to be there to take care of me, ought you not?"

"If you go away this time, Nell," he says, "some other man will fall in love with you, and you will never come back to me any more. I can see it all quite plainly. Will you not stay, dear, and try to put up with a poor, rough fellow *who loves you?*"

"There is no fear of any one I shall see there," I say softly; "besides, who is likely to fall in love with me there or anywhere else? Every eye has its own Naboth's vineyard (Did not some one or other say that?), and I am yours, but I'm not likely to be anybody else's. I shall come back again like a bad penny, never fear." I stoop to pluck a handful of small bind-weed, whose pale pink cups are opening to the sunshine with a dim faint fragrance.

"If only I were sure of you," says the young man; "if only these wretched months were up!"

"Poor George!" I say gently. Alas! that I should have to say, Poor George! When a woman pities her lover, she is a long, long way from loving him. I think he knows it, for he shakes his shoulders back impatiently; he looks as nearly wretched as his blonde, sunny good looks permit; these fair men never manage to look as disconsolate and woe-begone over their misfortunes as do the black-eyed, black-haired, funereal lovers.

In these morning rambles we always visit every outbuilding and corner, clean or unclean. We have now arrived at the pigsty, and the two papas are inside, prodding the fat sides of the porkers, and disputing loudly over the superiority of this breed or that. "Poor chucky!" I say, resting my elbows on the top of the stone wall that overlooks his unsweet dwelling, "you must have disagreed very seriously with our ancestors before they decided that your savoury body was unfit for food. Do you think," I ask, turning to George, "that they had trichinosis in those days?"

"Probably, only they called it by a less grand name!"

"The pigs must have had an excellent time of it when there was no one to eat them, you know; not that I will ever believe the Irish abjured the sweet creatures. I got into such a scrape here once," I continue, looking across to where the Mummy and the governor are waxing warm over their discussion. (After all a pigsty is not a very dignified place to quarrel in.) "Dorley used to milk a particularly vicious cow just in this corner; and one afternoon I popped my sun-bonneted head suddenly over the wall, and away went the cow, kicking over the stool, milk-pail, and Dorley, who lay on his back, with the milk all sweeling over him, never offering to move or get up, but just turned up the whites of his eyes, and murmured, ''Ow could'ee do it, Miss Ullen? 'ow could'ee do it?' What a row there was about it to be sure!"

I go off into a fit of laughter, in which George joins, and the two old people, having settled their dispute without coming to fisticuffs, move on, and we follow. How miserable it all is without Jack! Going over these old haunts without him; I feel almost as ancient as the "oldest inhabitant" does when he toddles round the house where he was born. It seems quite a century since we sat, one at each end of yonder plank, see-sawing, and tumbling flat on our noses five times in every minute. "I wonder what poor, dear Jack is doing?" I say aloud; "working himself to death I dare say! It was very inconsiderate of him, choosing a profession; there was no need, as he is the eldest son!"

"Jack is a lucky fellow," says George,

with a quick envy in his voice, " don't be sorry that he is not here idling his time away! He is out in the world making his life, or marring it; he has the chance of proving himself to be of good stuff or bad; he is not laid on a shelf like an old maid's gown, with sprigs of lavender between. Pythagoras says that, ' in this theatre of man's life, it is reserved only for God and angels to be lookers on;' and Arnold exclaims, ' Have we not all eternity to rest in?' Depend on it, Nell, every man ought to work."

"But what could you do?" I ask gently, for do I not know how this purposeless, idle life chafes him. "I don't think you are clever enough to cut a good figure in Parliament, and you would not care to be a clergyman or a doctor? If you had gone into the army as you intended, your time would have been filled up, but it would only have been like playing at being busy, for we never have any real fighting now, you know; we only make faces at our enemies, and show them that we are ready, and they never come on." George laughs.

"There are other things in the world besides fighting," he says, "plenty of good work to be done; but, however, it is no good talking about it. If ever I say anything to my father, he asks me if I shall not have time enough to do as I please after he is dead? Pleasant that!"

"After a certain age," I say gravely, "old people ought to go off; all that have any sense of propriety do, and make room for the young ones. They have had their day, cracked their jokes, drunk their wines; and when their lives are flat, stale, and unprofitable, they ought to make their bow and vanish."

"Only they don't think so," says George, laughing, "and Debrett chronicles many a depraved and inconsiderate old man, at a good deal past the orthodox three-score years and ten! and whose heir will have suffered the sickness of hope deferred, and have grown-up sons and a purple nose before he comes into his inheritance!"

"At any rate, George, you may be thankful that you are not a woman, shunted on to a siding, and bound to remain there for the rest of your life, unless some one has a fancy for murdering you, or you distinguish your-self in some discreditable way!"

"Women ought to be seen, but never heard of," says George, decidedly; "you don't want to scream on hustings, do you, Nell?"

"No, indeed, women possess far too much power to wish to wrest the semblance of it from man. A woman's rights! woman always seems to me to have lost all the privileges of her own sex, while obtaining none of the dignity of the other."

"Well done!" says George; "I'm glad you're not bitten like all the rest."

"That is because I am not clever," I say, laughing. "I should cut but a sorry figure among those highly cultivated females, and no one likes to look small!" (I turn aside to gather a spray or two of sweet woodruff that has no scent in life, but when dried possesses the fragrance of new-mown hay.) "Do you see that vervain, George? It is said to make the company it is in gay and jocund; had we not better take some home for our fathers?"

"I don't think *you* want any," he says, looking at me; "I never saw such a merry little soul as you are; and the way you laugh!"

"I read somewhere the other day, that every laugh is a nail out of your coffin," I say gaily; "if that is true there cannot be *one* left in mine, can there? Don't try and take from me my poor little cheerfulness; trouble will come fast enough; it always does to very happy people. It is the croaking, grumbling, ill-used folk who get through life comfortably and make other people bear their burdens!"

"You would never laugh as you do if you were in love," says George; "you couldn't."

"I do laugh very loud," I say, considering; "almost as loud as the Bull of Basan?" George does not answer, he appears to be thinking; so if I expect to be assured that my laughter is always low and sweet, I am mistaken.

"Do you know," I say, feeling rather ruffled, "that you never pay me any compliments now? No one ever paid me any but you, and, besides amusing me, I got quite to like them!"

"When a man is profoundly in love he does not make pretty speeches," says George; "he feels them, but he does not speak them. It would be like saying to the sun, 'How warm you are!' when he is warmed through and through with its rays. I don't think I ever paid you *compliments*."

"George," I say presently, as we walk noiselessly over the close-cropped, sweet meadows, "do you not think that a woman may have several fancies and only one heart? or do you believe her heart and her fancy always go together?"

"What put that into your head?" he asks, opening his eyes.

"Nothing!" I answer dreamily, "only I can understand a man and woman falling out terribly, because he thought she loved some one better than she did him, when in reality her heart belonged perfectly to that man, although a fleeting fancy for some one else had for the time being obscured her vision: there would be misery and confusion come, would there not? But after all it is the heart that stands, the fancy dies away like a puff of summer wind."

"Have a fancy for who you like, dear," says George; "only keep your heart for me!"

"If ever I had a fancy for any one," I say, looking out at the far away, bloomy hills, "I think it must have been in dreamland. Bah! we are talking nonsense. Do you know that I shall look such an old guy, if I go away? look at this frock!" And I hold out the skirt of my modest garment for his inspection.

"Well! and what is the matter with it?"

"Everything! material, fashion, cut, and age!"

"Never you mind!" he says, looking at my face, not my gown. "People will look at *you*, not your dress!"

"Not they!" I say, shaking my head. "Women look at your dress first and your face after; men look first at a woman's general turn out; they would rather be seen with an ugly but perfectly appointed woman, than ever such a pretty one in a bonnet out of date and ill gloved and booted."

"I should prefer the pretty woman with the out-of-date bonnet," says George; "but surely you can have everything you require for a visit?"

"I ought, but ought is an ill-used word that never gets its rights. Papa's daughters are never supposed to require anything so superfluous as *clothes*."

"If you would only marry *me*, you should have a new silk dress for every day in the year," says the young man, with masculine ignorance of the number of yards every well-brought-up young woman considers it necessary to cram into a skirt.

"You would not have me marry you for the sake of silk dresses, would you?" I ask reproachfully, feeling somewhat allured, nevertheless, at the notion of trailing about in black, white, green, blue, lilac, cream colour, or pink attire every day. I could not enjoy them all, though; and perhaps, after a bit, I should even get as used to them as I am to my cotton ones; and it would be no pleasure to choose a new one. "Heigho!" I sigh; "well, there is one comfort, I shall not have any of the women abusing me for my smart toilettes; a woman will forgive another one for being better looking than herself—that is Nature's fault, not her own—but she will never forgive her for being better dressed!"

"That is true," says George, "and I believe that numbers of people do not dare to be stylish, or they would lose all their friends. There is to some folks a species of immorality in a perfectly fitting dress or a becoming bonnet; it is a snare, a lust of the eye, and as such to be shunned by honest, sober people! I have often seen a man looking with positive pleasure at his dowdy, ill-dressed wife; it gives him a comfortable feeling of safety, to think that he can put her down in the middle of a crowded public room, and be certain to find her there unmolested when he comes back. In fact, too much style is the devil (they think), and men are often afraid to marry a very pretty or elegant girl, because they think her morals cannot be quite what they should be, or that she will take too much trouble in looking after!"

"And I have heard that a girl can have

no higher compliment than the dispraise of her own sex, and that when you hear them abusing and picking to pieces some particular woman, and assuring each other that she has not a good feature in her face, that her figure is padded, her complexion kept in a box, and that not even her eyelashes are her own, you may be quite sure she is good looking, or fascinating, or uncommon; on the other hand, if you hear them praising some girl to the skies, you may be perfectly sure that she is meek, insipid, and tame, too uninteresting to be a rival, and too vapid to attract the attention of any one's lover, husband, or brother.   Is that true?"

"Perfectly."

"Well, I can't understand that feeling. When I see anything beautiful, I love to look at it.   I never used to weary of looking at Alice or Silvia Fleming."

"Silvia Fleming!" he exclaims, "where did you ever see her?"

"At Charteris."

"At the time Vasher was there?"

"Yes."

"Whew!" whistles George; "why he

was in love with her; engaged to her some
years ago; no one ever knew why the
match was broken off. Vasher must be
getting an old fellow by now."

"Old!" I say in astonishment. "Old! did
you say? He cannot be much past thirty."

"That is a good deal," says George, with
all a young man's impertinence; "why, you
were only a child when you first knew him,
Nell?"

"Yes, I was only a child!"

"And I can't imagine how you recollected
him when you ran up against him in that
field."

"It is not a face one could possibly
forget," I say, rather tartly; "Paul Vasher
is the handsomest man I ever saw!"

George stares at me blankly; he does
not mind my not appreciating his good
looks, but it cuts him for me to place
another man before him.

"You always admired dark men," he says,
with a fall in his voice.

"Always!" I say, beginning to laugh.
"Do you know what I am laughing at?"

"No."

"I was thinking of that day when you were so angry, and walked off in a huff, and never turned your head once. I have so often thought since, that—that if you had only looked round, you would have seen how silly I looked when I ran into Mr. Vasher, and the moral I deduced was, 'never turn your back on your friends, but keep your eyes wide open to see when they make fools of themselves?'" And I laugh heartily; I always had a bad knack of laughing more amusedly at my own small jokes than those of anybody else.

We are in the orchard now, and the Mummy is beckoning from afar to George to accompany him home to luncheon, for above all earthly considerations does he place his stomach and the comfort thereof.

"Good-bye," says George, standing bare-headed under the trees, through which the sunlight flickers lovingly on to his fair, bright locks. "If you do go, which I devoutly hope you will not, Nell, there will be plenty of time for another nice long talk, will there not?"

"Plenty!" I say, my heart sinking, for

I know he will try and win an unconditional promise from me before I go, and that I never will give. " Good-bye, George ! "

And so he goes away, through the light and shadow, a stalwart, knightly figure that many a proud woman might look after with glad eyes of love and pleasure.

" O ! love, love ! " I say to myself as I go on towards the house, "that some people eat their hearts out in trying to win, and others take as thanklessly as though it were dirt; why do you not go where you would be welcomed with eager, grateful hands, instead of beating at a fast-shut door that can never be opened to you, never, ah ! never ! "

CHAPTER III.

"If thou art rich, thou art poor;
For, like an ass whose back with ingots bows,
Thou bear'st thy heavy riches but a journey,
And death unloads thee."

IT is Saturday, the thirtieth of August, and I am speeding along through golden sun-flooded fields of wheat, and shorn brown-green meadows; not on my own two indifferently shod feet, but in a carriage drawn by a puffing, snorting, hissing, dirty monster, who makes a prodigious noise, and hurry, and fuss, as he goes on his iron way rejoicing. I am off! Actually off! I am still doubtful as to whether it is really my veritable body that is seated on the hard blue cushions of the railway carriage. I keep on rubbing my eyes to be quite sure that I am awake, that I shall not find myself sitting up in bed, bitterly sorry and wrathful that a mocking dream has made a fool of me again. I have pinched myself hard six times, and at the end of each nip have felt relieved on finding that the train, my *vis-à-vis*, and my novel have not vanished into thin air. For a week I have been dancing like a cat on hot bricks, alternating between feverish hope and grovelling despair; I have packed and unpacked my modest wardrobe at least twelve times, and only a short hour ago, I was drowned in tears because the latest verdict had gone forth, " She shall not go." Whether mother thereupon went down on her knees before her lord, as Philippa did to hers, and softened his flinty heart with her tears and prayers, I know not; at any rate his decision was reversed, and that delusive jade Hope spread her wings and vanished, leaving blessed and calm certainty in her place.

It is a quarter of an hour since I left Silverbridge station, and wished mother and George good-bye. He did look so down in the mouth, and I always did hate to see a man miserable: all women whimper

more or less, but men ought not to be
bothered. Well, he'll get out into the
world some day, I hope; and there's nothing
puts a love affair out of a man's head so
quickly as having a lot to do: it is only
the people who sit down and think, think,
think, of one particular person, who take
a disappointment so much to heart. I think
most lunatics in love lived in the country.
I wish I had a pleasant travelling companion; some one who would not be afraid
to open his or her lips, and with whom I
could exchange a few reasonable remarks.
There is small hope, however, of this lot.
They belong, I can see at a glance, to that
large class of people who look with horror on
the smallest approach to conversation from
a stranger; who are bound hard and fast
by that ridiculous law of society which
commands human beings to be in each
others company for hours, and yet give no
more sign that they are aware of each
other's presence and existence than if they
were carrots or cabbages, or tables or
chairs; you may know who they are, and
they may know who you are, but until the

magic words of introduction have been spoken over you—they are not. You are voiceless, eyeless, earless; so are they, and nothing short of your being all jumbled up together in a horrible accident would give any one back their faculties. To this class of people, the offer of the smallest civility, a newspaper, a book or any other trifle, is regarded with grave doubt, and you are suspected of having designs on their purse, their bodies, or their acquaintance. "Nothing for nothing," is their motto. They never give without receiving a fair return, and why should *you!* It looks queer, to say the least. Therefore, when you are travelling, if you wish to be considered respectable, and neither an adventurer or adventuress, put on a stony countenance; look at the ceiling or your boots—never at the countenances of your fellow-travellers; receive any offer of book, paper, etc., with a haughty " Sir! " or " Madam! " look down your nose if any one address you : but to be pleasant, to say " Thank you! " and discuss the state of the weather, the state of the country, and the last new murder—then indeed you are low, hopelessly low, and you have yourself to thank if the silent ones dub you as something rather different to what you suppose yourself to be.

Now I should, above all things, like to ask one of those little virgins yonder to lend me the *Graphic;* there is a lovely picture in it, and I always did like pictures. I should like to announce publicly, that I am burningly, consumedly, unbearably hot; not but what my looks sufficiently attest the unwelcome fact, but it is always such a relief to talk over one's misfortunes; half mine always vanish when I can get any one to sympathize with me over them. In this case, however, I might be burnt to a cinder before I should dare to comment on the fact.

The two little people sitting opposite me are sisters, as alike as two peas, and I think as green; and the only difference that I can discern between them is that one has a permanent hitch in her nose, and the other has not. They are neither very young, nor very old: they hover on that chilly neutral-gray border-land that divides the young maid from the old one; they look as if they had never had a lover, or a sorrow, or a joy, or a hope, or a disappointment. I wonder what it feels like to have a torpid existence like that? Even the poor flies get wakened up and warmed by the sun sometimes.

A stolid British matron sits on my right, with a red account-book in her hand filled with rows of figures that should make her eyes ache. If ever I have a husband, I will take care of two things: that he keeps the accounts, and orders the dinner.

The only cheerful people present are two fat clergymen—comfortably dressed, happy, well-shaven souls, who are not only pleasantly provided for in this world, but are blessedly safe for the next. One is telling the other the latest *bon-mot* of a certain witty bishop, and I strain my ears to catch the pregnant syllables; but he laughs so much over it, that the point is lost in successions of chuckles, and I feel unreasonably though distinctly cross. The other man says, "Hey?" at every tenth word. It strikes me he must spend a good half of his waking existence in saying, "Hey?"

What a small insignificant person a spinster travelling alone looks! She is a poor creature, compared with the "married woman," and all her smart paraphernalia, the footman, the lady's maid, the nurse, the baby, the husband. I place him last of all, advisedly; for, though he provided all the rest, he is often the meekest and most unimportant of all.

No wonder men call themselves lords of creation! It is not for what they are, but for what they give, that they are of so much importance: all good things come to a woman through a plain gold circlet, apparently!

There is no denying it—I like to feel important; or rather, I think I should if I ever got the chance—for I never had one yet. I do not want to be married for years and years; but if I could have all the nice, pleasant, dignified surroundings that married women have, without being obliged to take the husband, I should *like* it. Now, if I happen to get smashed-up to-day, there is no one to gather my pieces together, or acquaint my friends of my demise, or give me decent burial. I shall be simply an unattended, unappropriated female, and of no account whatever. I am proud to say that I do not bear a bandbox, a bag, and a sheaf of umbrellas and parasols, as is the wont of most unmarried females : I have only one bonnet, and that is in my box, and in a bad way, I fear; for finding the trunk would not close, I sat down on the contents with much vigour, forgetting the bonnet in my excitement ; and to-morrow morning I shall be a sorrowful sight to see. We wanted to buy a new one—mother and I; but an empty purse stared us sternly in the face, and forbade the purchase. Next to being very hungry, I wonder if there is any misfortune, short of death, equal to that of an empty purse? To be ill in body is bad, to be ill in mind is worse, but for real downright, biting unpleasantness, and bitterness of soul, commend me to the empty pocket ! I fancy

Nick hates to see us penniless as heartily as we hate to see ourselves: he knows it is so easy for us to get into mischief when we have gold, so hard to distinguish ourselves in his court without it. I wonder how many extravagances and naughtinesses have been nipped in the bud for lack of the glittering dross? Well, if I do possess a sneaking love for smart clothes (is not love of dress one of his distinct and evil promptings? does he not ruin body and soul by hundreds every day, for the sheen that lies on a satin, the lustrous bloom on a silk, and the fairy cobwebs of a priceless lace?) it is pretty plain I cannot indulge it.

How hungry I am! In the breathless hurry-skurry of my departure sherry and sandwiches found no place: I was too intent on conveying my person and box to the station (anticipating a revoke of the favourable sentence) to think of probable hunger; now, as the train slowly glides into Pringly station, the sight of the refreshment bar, with its fossil sandwiches, leaden buns, and orange-coloured decanters, rejoices my heart.

"Guard," I say, jumping up as that individual goes past the carriage with his flag under his arm, "will you get me some sandwiches, and two buns, and a glass of ale, please?"

"Yes, miss,"—and he vanishes.

In my hurry I have trodden heavily on the foot of one of the elderly young ladies, and she gives me a look as I make my apologies that quite revives me, it is so healthily vicious. They exchange glances of horror out of their pale eyes as I drink Bass's best or worst. In all their lives, if their complexions may be trusted to speak truth, they have never tasted anything stronger than barley-water. Now, why drinking a glass of ale in a railway carriage when you are burnt up with dust and thirst, and scrammed with hunger, should be any worse than drinking ale at the family table when you do not particularly want it, I cannot understand; nevertheless, the British matron, the divines, and the little elderlies all look at me with shocked eyes. If they only knew how I am inwardly laughing at them! for is not this one of those little affectations that make one smile at human nature?

Away we go again, tearing through the bright beautiful country as though it were the desert of Sahara, and we could not leave it behind fast enough. How the sun pours down on our devoted heads! Truly August is giving us some straight burning strokes before it goes. How I fuss, and fidget, and fan myself, and adopt the hundred and one flapping and fussy measures that mortals suffering under discomfort always affect, until they resign themselves to the inevitable, and learn that hardest of hard lessons—endurance. The little females sit white and silent: they are very warm, they are suffering horribly, but they make no complaint. Somehow they irresistibly remind me of little boiled hens with melted butter poured over them. They do not grumble even to each other. Now if Dolly were here, I should keep up a never-ending stream of nouns and adjectives, and grow cool over the comfort I received. The British matron has closed her eyes, the account-book has slipped from her fingers, and she is asleep, giving utterance now and again to a majestic snore, that once or twice wakes her up, when she looks round fiercely at us all as who should say, " Who made that noise? I did not," and then goes off again.

The fat parson is no longer saying, " Hey? " aloud, though he may be shouting it in the land of Nod; his flabby cheeks are damp and unbeautiful, his mouth is a long, long way open. As a rule, human beings do not look well asleep: there is a startling resemblance between them and the ruminating animal world when the brain is dormant and the soul away.

After a while I think I fall off into a doze like the rest. I am conscious of making a deliberate effort to keep my mouth shut when " Luttrell! Luttrell! " comes sweetly to my ear. I start up in prodigious excitement, dancing up and down on both the little females' feet this time, but in too great a hurry to apologize; in fact, I am out of the carriage and across the platform almost before the train has stopped.

There is Milly in her carriage, but an

ampler, grander, different Milly somehow to
the bouncing, short-haired, handsome sister
of the old days.

"How do you do?" I say, rushing up to
her. "How glad I am to see you!" And
I give her a hug, for I have not seen her
for a long, long while.

"I am so glad you have come," she says;
"but good heavens, Nell! *what a hat* you
have got on!"

The gladness dies a little out of my face
and voice; I feel ruffled and vaguely chilled.
I have not seen her since her marriage, and
she might have looked at my face, not my
hat; besides, under the shadow of just such
an one has Milly walked for all the years of
her life before she married. As we drive
away she asks for all at home kindly enough,
but already I think her husband and child
fill her heart, and the pomps and vanities
and gauds and pleasures of her new life have
shouldered away the memory of the old one
at home. As I look at her I marvel if she
ever could have dodged papa round corners
and gone water-cressing, or worn a sun-
bonnet and double skirts? And although

I shut my eyes tight and try to conjure up the vision, I cannot.

"Where is Alice?" I ask. "I thought she would have come with you?"

"Charles is driving her this afternoon, but she will be in by the time we reach the Court."

"I am longing to see the babies," I say, looking at Milly's dress, and thinking what uncommonly fine birds fine feathers will make. (I am sure I could be made very presentable.)

"Mine is a splendid boy," says Milly, warming up directly: "he has the Luttrell skin and hair, and his eyes——" Words fail Milly at this point.

"And Alice's?"

"The youngest is a nice child."

"How droll it seems to think of Alice as a mamma with two children! And I have never seen the last one yet."

"Have you many people staying with you?"

"Not many—a dozen or so. There is Fane!"

We are in the park now, and across the

grass comes a tall, bonny, fair-haired young
fellow, with a sunshiny face and a bright
manner that makes every heart warm to
him. It was but little that I saw of him
at Milly's wedding; I am glad to have the
chance of knowing him better.

"I am so glad you have come," he says
heartily; "we were afraid that——"

A glance from Milly at the servants
checks him, and he jumps into the carriage
and we bowl away. I wonder if all married
people behave as these do? There they sit
face to face, hand locked in hand, gazing
at each other with an absorbed spooniness
that I do not know whether to smile at
or admire. Well, I don't wonder at her
loving him. In another minute we are at
the house and in the hall. Through the
half-opened drawing-room door comes a
sound as of many tongues, a chinking as
of many tea-cups; evidently all the world
is there.

"I will go to my room, thank you," I say
in answer to Milly's question. "Your maid
will show me the way."

As I mount the wide staircase, shallow

and wide enough to drive a coach and six down, I heave a deep sigh of relief. I am tired, hot, dusty; but oh! I am at my journey's end, and I am here, not at Silver-bridge. My room is vast, and wide, and cool; it looks over garden and pleasaunce, hill and dale, fashioned after nature's rarest and most lovely pattern; and away to the left glitters my splendid old friend, the sea, upon whose face I have not looked for many a long day. I have removed my travelling dress and am drinking tea, when Alice comes in with a rush.

"How delighted I am to see you!" she says; and we fly towards each other and kiss heartily.

"You disgraceful young woman!" I say, holding her at arm's length; "so you have been and had another baby, have you?"

"Is it not shocking?" she says, laughing. "I have my hands full, I can tell you."

"And what is the last one like?" I ask with interest; "as pretty as the first was?"

"Prettier!" says Alice, with emphasis.

"And what is Milly's like?" I ask, slyly.

"Oh, all very well; but he does not come up to mine."

(I expect some fun out of these babies.)

"And you are better looking than ever," I say, concluding my lengthened survey; "may I ask if you find any improvement visible in me?"

"Now I come to look at you," says Alice, "you are—yes—you decidedly are less plain than you used to be. There was a time, Nell, when I simply trembled for you, but your hair is lovely, your eyes are good, your dimples are charming. I think you'll do."

"Thank you," I say, meekly; "it is a case of 'it might have been worse,' is it not? Now, would you believe it, but I know a young man who thinks me *very pretty indeed?*"

"A young man!" says Alice, opening her eyes; "not in Silverbridge, surely? Did you advertise for him, or was he dropped out of a balloon?"

"Neither," I say, laughing; "but I am not going to tell you anything about him. I know so well how everything filters through to the husbands with married women, and I'm not going to have my heart's best affections made the theme of your unfeeling jokes. Did you think I should come, Alice?"

"Not in the least! Charles and Fane have been making bets on you. After this I shall expect you to come and stay with me at Lovelace Chace."

"I wish I could," I say devoutly; "but, this 'outing' over, I expect to be shut up for the rest of my days."

"Marry," says my beautiful sister, resplendent in all the pride of her matronly young beauty; "you will be able to do as you please then. Now—about this young man——"

"I won't tell you now," I say, putting my fingers in my ears. "I am so glad to have got clean away from him, you know; another day I will. Are any nice people staying here, Alice—any one I am likely to fall in love with?"

"What a question!" says Alice, opening her eyes. "If you think of doing any such thing, there is no need to talk about it beforehand, is there?"

"In this case," I say, seriously, "there is a great deal of need, for if I do not fall in love with some one within the next five months——"

"What then?"

"What, indeed?" I say, gaily. "Come now, tell me, have you any Prince Charming staying here?"

"There is one handsome man," says Alice, "Sir George Vestris; but he is in love with somebody; and there is little Lord St. John, whose possessions are charming if he is not, but *he* is in love with me; there are two detrimentals looking out for heiresses, and there is some new man who arrived this afternoon, whom I have not yet seen. It is very odd, he lives near Silverbridge—I can't remember his name. Fane and Milly knew him abroad. I am told he is good-looking."

"And this other man, the one you mentioned first, who is he in love with? Any one here? I should fall quite naturally into my character of *gooseberry* again."

"With the loveliest woman I ever saw," says Alice, "and she has a pretty name—Silvia Fleming."

"Silvia Fleming!" I cry, starting up, "are you joking?"

"Why should I be?" asks Alice. "Why, the Flemings *live* only twenty miles from here, and it seems Luttrell *mère* and Fleming *mère* were old friends; Fane asks them here every year."

"What a little place the world is!" I say, sighing; "how one does run up against everybody."

"But where did you ever meet with her, Nell?"

"Did I never speak of her? At Charteris."

"Ah! I remember. Well, she is a lovely bit of china, but I can't endure her."

"You are jealous," I say, looking at her proudly.

"Oh no!" she says, laughing, and in her voice there is the ungrudging admiration that one very pretty woman can always afford to give another; it is only your half-and-half beauties who deny the existence of anything comely in their fair neighbours— "but somehow I can't like her. There is something so silent, so secret about her, one never feels sure of what she is up to."

"And she is engaged to this Sir George Vestris?"

Alice shrugs her shoulders. "They are inseparable, they behave like engaged lovers; she takes no notice of any other man, and he is quite in earnest; but she, I believe, is amusing herself. Milly is considerably scandalized, Fleming *mère* shakes her head and says nothing, the young woman keeps her own counsel, and we are all in the dark."

"I wish she was married to him," I say, heartily.

"Do you, indeed?" says Alice. "May I ask, Nell, if you have any intentions on any one who admires her?"

"No intentions," I say, turning my head away that she may not see how red my face has grown, "but I think she is dangerous—a man-trap!—and the sooner matrimony locks her up the better."

"I must go," says Alice, jumping up as the sound of a distant bell comes to our ears. "Come into my room on your way downstairs, dear—it is the next but one on the right—and I will take you into the nursery to show you baby."

"Wait a moment," I say, running after her. "I never was a gusher, you know, Alice; but oh, I am so glad to see your pretty face again!"

I put on my white silk gown and twist a string of dim moonshiny pearls among my brown locks; I clasp about my throat and neck mother's pearl necklace and bracelets, and when all is done, survey myself in the mirror with sneaking admiration. "You little fool!" I say, shaking my fist at my pleased face; "you don't look so much amiss there all by yourself, but wait till you get downstairs among the rest—that'll take the conceit out of you!"

CHAPTER IV.

"A man that fortune's buffets and rewards
  Hast ta'en with equal thanks ; and blessed are those
  Whose blood and judgment are so well commingled,
  That they are not a pipe for fortune's finger
  To sound what stop she pleases."

In the Luttrell drawing-rooms, that open
one out of the other, almost as lofty and
wide as the aisles of a church, and which
are darkly splendid with the pictures of the
old masters and bright with glowing, brilliant flowers, that bloom in every nook and
corner like jewels set in dull brown leaves,
are sitting a dozen or so of people, enduring
that *mauvais quart d'heure* that precedes
dinner. Silvia has not yet made her appearance, but all the other guests are present,
I think, and I have bowed to so many, that
my head feels like a pendulum that is bound

to go on wagging by the force of its own momentum.

Mrs. Tempest reclines in an easy chair, fatter, kinder, fairer than ever—an agreeable contrast to the lady to whom she is talking, who is sallow and lean and ill-favoured. Her name is Lister, and she is mother to those two sweetly simpering young ladies who are frisking on yonder *causeuse* like lambkins, displaying an ostentatious affection for each other that speaks volumes for the encounters they have in private. Their nods and becks and wreathed smiles are evidently directed at two good-looking captains sitting near, who appear very insensible, and make no amative grimaces in return.

These latter are, I suppose, the detrimentals of whom Alice spoke. I like their clean, well-groomed looks much; they are the first "warriors bold" I ever saw, and they certainly seem to fulfil the whole duty of man, as understood by the youth of the present century, which is to be dressed to perfection and have the best manners compatible with the fewest possible ideas.

Talking to Alice is an ugly little fair man, who is looking at me through his eyeglass with attention, for do I not live near the rose?

Charles Lovelace, handsome as ever, a trifle steadier than he was on that terrible day when he ran away with Alice (and we wretched left behinds were left to pay the piper), lounges beside my chair, giving me little historiettes of the people present.

Leaning against the mantel-piece is a rather tall, very dark man, with a perfectly handsome face, that does not give me the impression of being particularly sensible or wise. That is Silvia's lover. She seems to have a rare taste for dark men, but this one does not to me approach or touch the grander, more masculine good looks of that other, who could renounce his heart's desire rather than forfeit his own self-respect. How strong and kind he looked when he said " Good-bye " to me under the porch at the Manor House! How surprised he would be if he knew both Silvia and I are here! I wonder if he has ever seen her since that Sunday at Flytton? I wonder if he will ever see her again?

I look up and see Paul Vasher coming in at the open door. My heart seems to stop beating as he comes forward. Are my eyes playing me some trick? Am I dreaming? No; for he comes straight to my side after Milly has introduced him to Alice (apparently he has seen all the rest this afternoon), and holds out his hand with a quick look of gladness.

"I had no idea I should see you here, or that you were Mrs. Luttrell's sister! Did you know that I should be here too?" he says, as he takes a chair next me.

"No, indeed!" How small my voice sounds! How tongue-tied I always am before this man!

"I hope you left all well at home?"

"Quite well, thank you."

(Is Silvia ever coming? It only wants one minute to eight.)

"Do you know," I say, rather nervously, "that you will see an old friend presently— or perhaps you have seen her already?"

"Do you mean Miss Fleming?" he asks quietly. "No, I have not seen her yet."

The door opens and enter Silvia. As she comes up the long rooms I see her clearly enough, a thought larger, a shade more voluptuous than she used to be—a woman now, not a girl. She wears dead white silk, with costly lace at breast and elbow, and faint golden yellow roses in her hair and the front of her gown. Her beauty strikes me as freshly and surprisedly as it did the first time I ever saw her.

Sir George Vestris goes to meet her with almost humble devotion, but she looks around her seeking, I think, Paul Vasher, and he rises and approaches her. They are so near me that I could touch either with my hand, and cannot choose but hear their words.

"How do you do, Miss Fleming?" says Paul.

"Quite well, thank you, Mr. Vasher."

"It is many years since we met," says the gentleman politely.

"It does not seem so long," says the lady.

"Dinner is served," announces the butler.

"Will you take in my sister, Mr. Vasher?"

says Milly; and I put my hand under his arm.

So this is the meeting after long years between these two once passionate, despairing lovers. Cold and indifferent as their words were, their looks matched them; not a ray of excitement or interest stirred Mr. Vasher's face, and she was no whit behind him, and yet methinks there must lurk some danger when two people who parted so wildly meet so coldly.

Somehow or other we are all matched; the stray men come out of their corners and fall in with the rest, and we go across the hall and into the dining-room, dim with wax lights, faint and subdued as a room devoted to the worship of the palate should be—or so gourmands tell us.

As yet, however, I am too young to love my dinner very heartily. As yet I " eat to live "; in the fulness of time I may perhaps " live to eat ", but not now, not yet! I would rather be out in the garden than sitting here watching unhungry people tempted with good things, and I want to be able to think. It is all so wonderful, that Silvia and Paul Vasher should have met again. Will it be my lot to see the last act played out, and the lovers, after all their misunderstandings, made happy?

"It is the oddest thing, my meeting you here," says Paul, as we sit down. "Did you know you were coming, when I wished you good-bye at Silverbridge?"

"I did not know it for certain myself until eleven o'clock this morning," I say laughing. "When I saw you last I never thought any such dissipation was likely to befall me as paying a visit."

"You have left your colour behind," he says, looking at me, "with the poppies."

"Those poppies!" I say, ruefully. "Oh! how good it was of you not to laugh!"

"I felt no inclination," he says; "the picture would not have been half so pretty without the flowers."

Here he betakes himself to his soup, for apparently he is hungry if I am not. Across the table, and plainly visible (for Milly's servants understand the art of arranging a dinner table, and no enormous épergnes and show pieces of plate make a wall to block out our opposite neighbour, compelling us to gaze at our plates or our right and left companion for several hours), are Silvia and Sir George Vestris—she flirting as lightly as though the man sitting before her had never been any more to her than any other present; he, with his soul in his eyes and words, watching her exquisite face as though his life hung upon her favour.

"Do you think she is altered?" asks Paul's voice beside me; and I turn with a start.

"She is more lovely, I think. I see no other difference."

He is looking at her with a glance that is most coldly critical. It has none of the suppressed intensity of the unwilling lover, or the open admiration of the enamoured one; it is simply and utterly indifferent. Verily a man's love passeth quickly. And yet I wrong Paul Vasher in this, for his love did not pass away; he wrestled with and cast it out.

"Do you know," he says, "that you are the quietest young lady I ever took in to dinner in my life? I have not heard the sound of your voice for quite——"

"A minute!" I say, laughing, "and those at home would tell you that is an enormous time for me. But I know men hate to be talked to at dinner. You look upon women as a nuisance in that respect, and would abolish us from the table altogether if you could; now, would you not?"

"Not when they are as considerate as you," he says, "although I will confess that I have before now got up from dinner as hungry as I sat down, thanks to my companion's conversational talents."

"But if *she* talked you were safe, surely? You need only have answered in monosyllables."

"Only, unfortunately, she had the finest knack of interrogatory conversation that I ever heard. She would ask questions that could not be answered ' in russet yeas and honest kersey noes.'"

"I should have feigned deafness," I say laughing. "She could not shout at you!"

There is a little pause while he helps himself to *vol-au-vent*, and I look round the room at the dark oak, at the massive sideboard, on which is carved the date 1690. How small and insignificant that date makes me feel, and how evanescent a thing life is. For how many generations has not that sideboard held food and drink? for how many more will it not hold the same? Just as those dead and gone Luttrells looking out from the canvas on the walls once sat here, jocund and happy, so will others fill up our places who are sitting here to-night, and these sober pictures will look down on them as benignly as they are looking on us. Stately old houses certainly lessen one's sense of self-importance. It is impossible in the face of the stored traditions and memories of many hundred years not to feel that these things remain, and *we go*.

I glance round the table. Mrs. Fleming is steadily laying the foundation for a fourth chin. Mrs. Lister is boring Fane to a pitch that almost brings tears into his eyes; he makes no secret of hating old women, and every night he is bound to take one in for his sins. Lord St. John is gazing at Alice, who is placidly eating her dinner; every one of us Adairs have fine appetites, and are not ashamed of them. Miss Lister is worrying Captain Brabazon, who is trying with secret wrath, I am certain, to eat *his* dinner. The other sister looks sulky; apparently her squire is better skilled in the art of repelling unwelcome advances than the other poor captain.

Ah me! I wonder why it should be that when lovers do not come to look for Chloe, Chloe should invariably go to look for them!

"Can you tell me who that gentleman sitting next to my sister is?" I ask Mr. Vasher.

"Silvestre of Melton. Do you like his looks?"

"He seems good-tempered," I say smiling, "and he is very amusing to listen to. His ideas seem to sprawl all over the place, and he requires his companion to pick them up and put them before his eyes in a recognizable form! Is he not very lazy?"

"Very," he says; "and are not you rather sarcastic?"

"Sarcastic!" I repeat, staring. "Where

could I have possibly picked up that trick? I only watch people, you know."

"And some day you will turn my character inside out, and hold it up for me to look at," says Paul.

"If you cannot hold your own against a village maid, I am sorry for you!" I say, slyly. "Does it not seem droll that Miss Fleming and you and I should all have met together again here? It reminds one of the witches' meetings in Macbeth—does it not you?"

"Only I trust we shall not work such disasters as they did!" he says laughing. "Do you know that I was in such a hurry to get back to Silverbridge, that I only came here intending to remain until Wednesday, but now I shall stay."

"So he loves her still," I say to myself, glancing at Silvia.

"Will you be glad or sorry?" he says, looking at me.

"I am glad you are going to stay," I say, "very glad. I will even, if you like, play gooseberry for you. There!"

I have made another mistake. He never

knew till this moment that I knew he was in love with Silvia. Having made the observation, however, I will not attempt to eat it: telling stories is so painful and hard, one had need to be so clever to fib successfully; and I never was clever, thank heaven!

"Gooseberry!" he says, with a swift amused gleam in his eyes; "for me and whom?"

I do not answer, for the sound of voices is ceasing, Milly is drawing on her gloves; and who cares to hear his or her witty or flattering remarks cut ignominiously short by an universal uprising of petticoats?

"And whom?" says Paul's eager voice in my ear, but I turn my head away with a mischievous smile. Milly is collecting the glances of her compeers now, and I leave my seat with the rest.

"You shall tell me by-and-by," says Paul decidedly, as he holds the door open for me to pass out last of all, behind the bashaw-like tails of my elders and betters.

"Do not be too sure," I say laughing. "And now," I think to myself, "for a time of penance. Women can be cosy enough together if they all know one another well, but a jumble of relations, friends, and acquaintances—never!"

Silvia has vanished when I reach the drawing-room. No one abhors her own sex more heartily than she, and I do not feel inclined to make friends with the sisters, who are sitting on a distant couch, chattering very earnestly, reporting progress no doubt. The matrons sit in a ring and discourse of babies and the extraordinary rascality of their servants, male and female. I am not married, and I have no servants, not even a lady's maid; so I turn my back on the drawing-room and go upstairs to the Lovelace and Luttrell nurseries, and look at the babies, happy little souls, with their perfectly blank memories, that enable them to sleep on and on and on, with nothing to awaken them save hunger. They look such soft, round little cherubs, with their tiny clenched fists touching their cheeks. I never can see a baby without pausing to dream over it, and recalling with an amazed wonder the fact that all our great heroes and statesmen and illustrious men were even thus once— yes, and our murderers, our felons, and our outlaws.

The young mothers and the others come up, and an enormous amount of baby worship is gone through, during which I slip away, and going to my room look out at the night and promise myself a stroll by the sea on Monday. I wonder why people always eschew the sea on Sundays? On the same principle as they make themselves uncomfortable in every imaginable way, I suppose.

We all go downstairs, and as I cross the drawing-room I see Silvia sitting by the window. She has not spoken to me yet, but then she has had no chance; I will go and speak to her.

"Have you forgotten me?" I say, putting out my hand. "I stayed with your aunt once at Flytton, you know; I am Helen Adair."

She looks at me for a moment, considering; then she lays her hand in mine. "You are Helen Adair?" she says, with a kind of amazement. "I thought I had seen you somewhere before, but I did not know it was at Charteris."

And as we stand hand in hand, the door opens and Paul Vasher comes in, first of the advancing party of men, and looks at us with a quick and keen scrutiny. In another minute Sir George Vestris is beside her, and I am sitting on a velvet chair, professedly looking at Milly's album; in reality wasting a little malicious pity on the Misses Lister, who, having laid themselves out in shady corners with room beside them for one, are baulked by Silvia, whose lovely face detains the captains on their enforced pilgrimage to those charmers. Has she not Sir George Vestris, and is it not mean of her to prevent those flies from walking into the parlours the spiders have so carefully prepared? Mr. Vasher comes and sits down beside me, taking half of the heavy book on his knee.

"Do not make fun of them," I say, laughing, "for nearly everybody here is a relation."

"Do relations love one another?" he asks. "If I wanted a real service done me,

or had got into a scrape, I would go to a
friend, not a man bound to me by blood.
Relations give ton-loads of good advice, and
there they stop."

"I never had any," I say; "and I always
have been so sorry that I had not. Why
should one always be getting into scrapes?"

"It is human nature," says Mr. Vasher.
"Now, does she not look a little duck?"

The "little duck" is our queen, and
the photograph represents her as she was
in her beautiful youth, with the gentlest,
prettiest, most lovable face in the world;
looking upon it one's heart aches as one
thinks of the long, dark, empty years that
came to her after these blessed and happy
early days. Her daughter-in-law looks from
the opposite page with her exquisite tender
smile. As Englishwomen beat all other
women, does not our princess beat all em-
presses, queens, and princesses with her
fair face? Our prince was in luck when he
went a wooing.

"Are you loyal?" I ask, looking up at
Paul Vasher; "I hope so, for I could never
like you if you were not. Some people say

rude things about royalty; they think it sounds grand, but *I* think it is simply very bad taste."

"Shall you think I am disrespectful if I say that in my opinion kings and queens are not as good-looking as every-day people?" he asks.

"No, for that is often true. For instance," I say, looking across at Silvia and her lover, "where would you see such a pair as that?"

He does not wince in the very least as his eye falls upon them, and yet he is going to stay on here for her sake.

"So that is the couple for whom you are kindly going to act the part of gooseberry?" he asks, with a smile. "I thought you said you were going to play it for me?"

"So I was," I say, turning very red, but still looking him well in the face; "it was you I meant."

"And the lady?"

"Look at this photograph," I say quickly; "is it not pretty?" In my hurry I have laid my finger down on a fat baby taken *à la* fig-leaf, so precipitately shift it and indicate a couple of Luttrell lovers, who look even more foolish than they feel.

"Very," says Mr. Vasher, with emphasis. "But where is the gooseberry?"

"I wonder," I say, raising my voice a little, that I may talk my colour down, "why plain people have their photographs taken so much oftener than handsome ones? It is such a rare thing to find a pretty face in an album. Do you think those people *know* how ugly they are?"

We are looking at a man whose eyes, already well rolled by nature, have evidently acquired a distinct and supererogatory roll by long practice; he looks as if a smart rap on the back of his head would send them into his lap.

"No," says Paul, "for the plainest people always think themselves the handsomest. Have you ever had yours taken?"

"Once, at Pimpernel; it was a horrid experience, and I never wish to have another like it."

"What did he do?" asks Paul. "Did he, like the little fat photographer in *Punch*, say, 'Look at *me*, miss, and don't smile?'"

"No, but he did worse; he *wished* me to smile, but he would not let me do it my own way—he regulated it. When I had got up a moderate grin, he would say, 'A little more, miss!' but on trying to oblige him I showed a little of my teeth, which was strictly forbidden. Then, when I had nailed a painful smile to my countenance, and at his command made an arch grimace with my eyes, he took the cap off, and it was a horrible thing to feel my smile slipping away from me, though I held on to it with my eyelids, and to know that it was going—going—gone!"

"I am afraid the Pimpernel process is a long one," says Paul, laughing.

While he puts the book back I glance around me. The men look amiable and cheerful in the extreme, as all mankind has a way of doing after dinner; one or two of them sentimental, tears will stand in their eyes by-and-by, if a plaintive ballad is sung. It is not an ennobling reflection that the best of men is better after a good dinner than he was before; and that the hottest lover can be made hotter still by a choice vintage. Miss Lister is going to sing; she spreads out her green skirts, and takes off her bracelets and clears her throat. Do the birds make any preparations before bursting out in a rush of exquisite song? She sings "Only," and Jack's ridiculous verse comes into my mind as I listen—

> "Only a face at the window,
>   Only a face, nothing more ;
>   If ever it owned any legs,
>   They must have walked out at the door."

Some songs move me, but this one never does. Give me "When sparrows build," with the yearning cry of the girl's broken heart wailing through it, and "the faded bents o'erhead." Alice sits down and plays glorious "Tam O'Shanter." How the rollicking, dare-devil, spirited notes ring out! How we seem to see the hot pursuit, feel the witch fingers creeping nearer and nearer to the terrified galloping horse! An hour slips away. It has been a charming evening.

"Good-night!" says Paul Vasher, standing before me ; "we are banished to billiards. Are you going to begin your duties as gooseberry to-morrow morning?"

CHAPTER V.

"He hath twice or thrice cut Cupid's bow-string, and the
little hangman dare not shoot at him : he hath a heart as
sound as a bell, and his tongue is the clapper; what his heart
thinks his tongue speaks."

IT is half-past eleven o'clock and we are all
in church (save Fane and Captain Oliver),
confessing ourselves to be miserable sinners,
although in our secret souls we think ourselves nothing of the sort. We are in a big
pew that contains, besides hassocks and
chairs, a carpet, a table, a cupboard, and
red curtains, which latter hide us when
sitting or kneeling from the open-mouthed,
open-eyed gaze of the Luttrell hinds. In
former and more unmannerly days the cupboard held good store of cake and wine, of
which the squire, his wife and daughters,
and the stranger within his gates, partook
during the sermon. Rather trying for the
poor parson overhead on a hot summer's

day, with his parched throat, and secondly, thirdly, and fourthly still before him.

And now we are all standing up, able to take our fill of staring at the well-washed, well-greased congregation, who are singing " Jerusalem the golden " with all the strength of their bucolic hearts and voices.

I wish they had a few H's among them, these good and bad people! They let them all go so recklessly, but with the universal law of compensation put them in again in the wrong place. How loud and clear presently sounds their " Incline our 'arts to keep this law ! " It is no use to struggle against overwhelming numbers; we may as well let ours go with the rest, for we can never leaven the lump. I think that whoever invented the letter H did not sufficiently take into consideration the prevailing tendency of mankind to ease. Aitch! It is a word in itself, and a hard one; in hot weather especially, how comfortably and easily does it disappear altogether!

The rector is very like Mr. Skipworth in appearance, voice, and manner. For an hour we sit under him and listen to his dis-

cursive ramblings, which, so far as I can
make out, are about Jeremiah in the briars,
though what on earth he did there and how
he got into such an uncomfortable position
we are not told. Could not a clever man
say all he has to say to his congregation
pithily and well in twenty minutes? Is
there anything that damages the cause of
Christianity so much as the incapacity of
these servants of God to expound the Scrip-
tures lucidly and well? In the Houses of
Parliament, and wherever enlightened men
are gathered together to hear clever, wise,
or improving talk, would they sit silent for
an hour listening to twaddle that is an
insult to their understanding? A thousand
times, no! They would walk out, or cry
aloud, or silence the speaker quickly
enough; but in the house of prayer that
cannot be done, and so folks with starving
souls go Sunday after Sunday seeking bread
and having a stone offered to them. Surely
men who stutter, men who speak indis-
tinctly, men whose hearts may be pure and
good enough, but whose words are weak;
men who have no strong sympathy with

their hearers, and cannot express themselves concisely and to the point—ought these men to be set up above their fellow-men, to preach the grandest, highest truths the world contains ? A man should be proved to be a good and bold orator, a sound logician and accomplished scholar, so that he may appeal as irresistibly to the mind and imagination as to the souls of his congregation, before he enters holy orders ; for is not an enormous power put into his hands for good or evil ?

When a fine preacher arises, how people flock from the north and from the south, from the east and from the west, to hear him ! How his fiery, heart-searching words pierce his listeners' hearts. How he holds the mirror up to the bad, wicked soul, and cries, " Behold ! to this you have fallen and are falling ! " We almost see the gaping bottomless pit, with the writhing scorpions and the worm that never dies ; feel the licking fire of the curling flames ; hear the voice of the Man of Sorrows calling us away from destruction. I heard such a man once at Pimpernel.

And now we are out again, and walking across the churchyard; and the sun flickers down gaily on the living who walk erect, and on the green shield of earth that lies heavy on the breast of those who have "fought their fight with the pale warrior," and been vanquished, as all men have been and must be. At the gate the carriages are waiting, for Luttrell Court is more than two miles away, and I find myself seated next to Mr. Vasher, and opposite Milly and Mrs. Lister.

"How well you behaved in church," says Paul; "you never smiled once, not even when that fat lady tried to pass the fat man in the narrow pew, and they got wedged together!"

"Did I not?" I say laughing. "I could not help thinking of a rhyme in one of the nursery books at home—

'There was a young lady of Yarrow
Who went up to church in a barrow.
She said with a smile,
As she stuck in the aisle,
They build these here churches too narrow.'"

"The lady in church must have been a direct descendant of the one at Yarrow," says Paul, looking at me.

I hope he is not observing the crushed and forlorn appearance of my bonnet; in future I will, at all risks, carry a band-box. Milly's airy erection is quite faultless. How good-tempered people ought to feel when they are perfectly well dressed! I could be quite angelic, I think, if I were. Mrs. Lister looks as prim and unapproachable as though she were made of buckram. Her lips are pursed up very tight; she grasps her prayer-book as though it were a pistol, and altogether she is not a pleasant object to contemplate.

"There is Fane!" says Milly suddenly, as we roll smoothly along under the shadow of the giant trees that line the park; and there, sure enough, in the distance, sneakily dodging behind a tree, and looking very hot, dirty, and ashamed of himself, is her missing lord and master.

Did I ever say that Fane is only a few years older than Milly, and that they are a very young couple indeed? Every Sunday morning, regularly as clockwork, does Milly make Fane dress to go to church with her, and every Sunday morning at the very last moment does he succeed in making his escape, and she has to go without him. This morning he has seduced Captain Oliver from the path of duty, and the pair have evidently been up to some unlawful amusement, for they appear exceedingly anxious to hide their persons from our view. But Milly gets out of the carriage and majestically walks across the grass to where they lie *perdu* (Where could she have learnt that dignified swagger? I should like to see her try it on with the governor), and we all follow.

Fane and his companion thus run to earth, emerge and present their disreputable persons to our gaze. Their light summer suits are all patched and stained with green, as though they had been rolling on the grass. The Captain's face is scratched, and so is Fane's hand. Half-a-dozen dogs are tearing round and round a tree, at the top of which a piteous miau! sufficiently explains the nature of these gentlemen's Sunday morning amusements.

"I am disgusted with you, Fane," says Milly; "and as to you, Captain Oliver, I am *surprised* at you."

And she sails away with her lord, leaving poor Captain Oliver utterly squashed. He does not know that it is Milly's habit to visit all her husband's misdeeds upon his friends, and that nothing will ever make her believe that they do not lead him into every scrape—not he them.

"Poor Oliver!" says Paul, as we walk away, leaving that abased warrior to the tender mercies of Mrs. Lister. Very tender they will be too, as she wants him for a son-in-law. "How crestfallen he does look, to be sure! And he is considered to have more brass than any other man in his regiment." . . .

"He is quickly routed, then; but it is impossible for a man to be rude to a lady, is it not?"

"Quite."

"Are fathers generally polite to their families?"

"If they are gentlemen."

"Oh!"

"I want to know," says Mr. Vasher, looking down on my tumbled bonnet, "what I am to call you. I won't call you Miss

Adair; I don't like Helen. May I call you Nell?"

"Oh no. What would Milly say? Besides, I was young when you used to call me that; I am grown up now."

"And no longer young?"

"Oh yes; pretty well. When we have known each other a little longer, you know——"

"Yes, we shall be near neighbours," he says, with quite a sudden gladness in his voice; "we shall have plenty of time for getting to know each other better."

"I do not improve on acquaintance," I say smiling. "Oh, you will find me out to be such a little wretch. If you saw me in a rage once you would not forget it."

"Who puts you out?"

"Dorley, or Basan, or—or—another person."

"And supposing I do?"

"You will be frightened."

"I am not afraid," he says, looking deep into my laughing face with his brown, brown eyes, that are self-willed and strong and tender at one and the same time.

"Did any one ever keep you in order, Nell?"

"Never!" I say, proudly.

And I smile to myself as I think of my lover and bond-slave George, who never swayed, never could sway me in will, or mind, or heart. No, certainly, I have never been managed by anybody yet.

"Women ought not to have their own way," says Mr. Vasher. "After a while they go in for Women's Rights, and at last it come to the husbands standing on the platform and holding the baby, while they hold forth upon everything in heaven and earth."

"I don't think those sort of people ever have anything so frivolous as a baby," I say, considering. "Talking of babies, do you know that you will see two at luncheon to-day? They are coming down for certain."

"Horrible!" he says, shuddering. "If there is one sight more appetizing, clean, and savoury than another, it is a baby at table."

"Take care the mothers do not hear

you," I say, as we enter the house; "they would never speak to you again."

We have taken off our bonnets and pulled out our locks, have powdered or not powdered our hot faces as our habits or inclinations will, and we are sitting one and all in the cool dining-room eating cold lamb and salad. The griffins outside shadow themselves grotesquely on the drawn blinds; they seem to grin in upon us malevolently, with their great misshapen noses and curling wicked mouths. Everybody is talking at once, eagerly, alertly, as though the loss of his voice for two hours had been a severe trial, and he is determined to make up for lost time.

"I saw a man in church who was even smaller than I am," says Lord St. John to me, "and I was so pleased. Not but what I always console myself with a couplet that I saw somewhere once; it began—

> 'Man wants but little here below,
> Nor wants that little long.'"

"I fancy that applies to things, not people," I say, doubtfully, "and I am nearly sure it is a hymn."

" St. John has lost himself among the Psalms," says Charles.

" The safest place he ever got into," says Mr. Silvestre.

" That comes of going to church," says Captain Brabazon.

Lord St. John smiles blandly at his friends and continues : " It may be that I am prejudiced, Miss Adair, for a man naturally likes to think that he ought to be exactly like what he is, but I like being little. There is a peculiar charm in the upside-downness of being a lord of creation, and yet so much shorter than most ladies—to feel that they could take me up and horsewhip me without an effort, and yet that they do not ! Delicious creatures ! And it is a fact, Miss Adair, that if ladies cannot have a gigantic slashing fellow for a lover, who could crush them between his finger and thumb, they like to have something that they can protect, and pet, and spoil. Women's love is divided into two classes, the adoring and the protective, and upon my word, I think the dear souls enjoy the one as well as the other."

There is a chorus of laughter all round the table, in which Alice joins. I wonder if *she* pets the little man?

He betakes himself to claret cup; so do I, and sit listening to the nonsense that is flying about. How very seldom Silvia's voice is heard. It is the rarest thing to hear her speak, and then it is only to Milly or Fane, or Sir George Vestris. Although she lives among us, she somehow seems to be set apart, if it were not for her perfect loveliness, one would never know she was present. I have seen neither look nor word exchanged between her and Paul Vasher to-day. If he loves her still, how can he bear to see her appropriated by another man as he does? Lovers are kittle cattle. The butler is opening a bottle of Bass leisurely; but some imp of the weather has got inside it, and he shoots out the corkscrew in the man's face, hitting him severely on the nose, and deluging him in frothing, foamy liquid. To his credit be it spoken, however, there is not the ghost of a smile upon his face, only ale, and he takes a cloth and wipes himself. Mr. Vasher catches my eye and laughs. I am glad he has some sense of the ridiculous; people are so diffi-cult to get on with who have none. I wish he was on my side of the table, and not all that way off. Mrs. Lister is opposite me, and I make a discovery concerning her; she wears false teeth and they do not fit her. She will choke herself some day. Perhaps if she were to return them to the dentist and say—

> "Take back the teeth that thou gavest—
> What is their use, sir, to me?"

he would give her a set that might fit her better.

"There's my precious," exclaims Alice, lifting her head and listening; and sure enough certain clucks and coos and chokes in the distance announce the advent of the olive branches.

The door opens and enter two nurses bearing aloft a small Lovelace and a smaller Luttrell, who are deposited by the same on their mothers' laps. Milly's baby is very young yet, and has that peculiarly decrepid look that extreme youth and age seem to share equally. His wonderful little hands are as shrivelled and wrinkled as though he had taken in washing for a hundred years. He is too small to be troublesome, and lies flat on his back, staring about him and taking a meal off his fists. Alice's son is a different matter. He is eighteen months old, and of an inquiring, avaricious turn of mind. He drinks wine out of his mother's glass without winking; he smashes a plate or two, and nearly puts out his eyes with a fork. He takes a fancy to some bright, golden coloured jelly before him, but when he has some on a plate does not eat it; only churns it all up between his fingers, becoming so absorbed in his occupation, that his voice is not heard for fully two minutes.

Little Lord St. John leaves his place, and goes round to look at the youngster, addressing it affectionately as " chucky, chucky, chucky!" whether under the mistaken notion that he is a species of young pig, I know not.

" Little angel!" murmurs Alice, gazing at her son.

" Pretty king!" says Milly, as her infant sneezes in her face.

"Never makes a sound," says Alice, kissing the top of her baby's golden head.

"Never cries at strangers," says Milly, rubbing her cheeks against her heir's primrose down.

I never knew until to-day how mothers *drivel*. Lord St. John ventures his face too near Alice's boy, and he puts out his plump, jelly-covered little fingers, and firmly grasps that gentleman's moustaches with a solemn and delighted countenance. The more the poor man tries to get away, the harder the baby holds on, and not until tears of pain stand in Lord St. John's eyes is he released. At the top of the table there is a sort of happy family show, that is calculated to fill all beholders with an insane desire to jump up and rush, all of us, to church and be married on the spot— the spectacle of connubial bliss is so beautiful. Fane looks at Milly, then at the baby; Milly looks at the baby, then at Fane. It is very touching, no doubt; but is it not rather public? Young Lovelace has struggled to the floor, and made friends with the dog. They are eating a biscuit between them. The dog takes a bit, then the baby does. It is very interesting, but rather dirty.

We go into the drawing-room, and stare at one another, and marvel, as everybody does every Sunday of their lives, what we are going to do with ourselves. If I were twenty years older I should retire to my bedroom and go comfortably to sleep, as Mesdames Fleming and Lister are going to do, I am morally certain. Alice and Milly have vanished after their babies; the Misses Lister are whispering together; Silvia is giving Sir George Vestris a liberal education at the window. A sound of merriment comes faintly from Fane's study; clearly men have a better notion of passing time than ladies. Reading novels on Sunday is forbidden, but it is no sin to *act* them. Spicy, full flavoured, exciting love-stories run through more quickly and easily on this day than any other, and more love nonsense is talked on a Sunday than in all the remaining six days of the week.

"Are you going to church this afternoon?" asks Paul Vasher's voice behind me, as I stand drumming my fingers against the glass.

"It is too hot," I say, turning round. "Oh, I do feel so cross! Why may not one work, or dig, or do something useful on Sunday afternoons?"

"We are going to church," says Miss Lister, appearing before us; "will you come, Miss Adair?"

"No, thanks," I say, looking up at the burning, cloudless vault overhead. "Is it not too far for you?"

They do not think it is, and go away to "put their things on," which means half-an-hour's hard labour before the looking-glass, trying to make a silk purse out of a sow's ear.

"Don't betray me if I tell you a secret," says Paul, laughing, "but I think the Listers expect Brabazon and Oliver to accompany them to church, and they are hiding."

"What cowards! Did they promise to go?"

"They temporized, I believe."

"Alas! for the glory of the British flag,"

I say, "is not that one of them peeping round the beech-tree?"

"It is."

"I have a great mind, a very great mind, to tell the Listers where he is; they would not stand on ceremony, they would *fetch* him."

"Brabazon and Oliver would run," says Paul, "and it is too hot for a chase, is it not? Here they are."

Yes, here are the young ladies freshly touzled, freshly repaired, with smart white veils that *now* stand out jauntily enough from their faces, but will by-and-by stick to them or melt imperceptibly into the same.

"Have you seen Captain Oliver?" asks the one.

"Have you seen Captain Brabazon?" asks the other, looking anxiously about.

They are not looking in the right direction, or they would see the whole of one gentleman's right boot and half of the other gentleman's left eye. They hunt about for a little while, poor souls, and at last, shame forbidding them to take their bonnets off, they set out across the park, quarrelling fiercely as they go, if one may judge by their backs. When the coast is clear the captains cautiously leave their hiding-place, and make off, looking as pleased as two school-boys.

"When I look at those girls," says Paul, emphatically, "I feel thankful that I have no sisters."

"I am going out into the garden," says Milly, appearing with Fane; "will you come, Nell?"

I fetch my hat, and we all go out together. Husband and wife walk on in front. His arm is round her neck, her arm is half-way round his waist; they lean towards each other like a tall and short weeping willow. It is rather trying to one's gravity to walk behind them, and, catching Paul's eye, I go off into a fit of laughter.

"Do they always behave like that?" I ask. "I never saw them together before, except when they were engaged, and there was some excuse then."

"They always did abroad," says Paul, "or at least when I met them; they were the amazement of all beholders."

"I would rather get up early in the morning to do it," I say energetically, "than have every one smiling at me, would not you?"

"Much rather!" he says, with emphasis; "it would pretty well take the bloom off to have any amount of people looking at one."

We are in the park now, where are cool shady paths and long pleasant glades, through which the hot tyrannical sun cannot pierce. In the distance Silvia and Sir George Vestris are walking; do they never, I wonder, grow tired of each other's society?

"There go the lovers," says Paul, looking towards them.

"Are they both pretending, do you think?" I say, speaking my thoughts, as I have a bad knack of doing since; for what are words given us, save to delicately disguise our meaning?

"Pretending!" he repeats, with real astonishment; "why should she? I did not know people ever pretended to be in love."

Evidently he has no suspicion that she loves him still; far less is there any of the quick eagerness in his voice that a lover should borrow.

"Nell," he says, looking down on me with a queer smile, "don't ever try to deceive any one, for your face will always betray you! Now, I know what you are thinking; pray, was it to me and *Silvia* that you meditated playing gooseberry?"

"Yes, it was," I say, turning my red face round. "I have always wanted to tell you. I knew all along that you *liked* her; I knew it at Charteris."

"And you think I *like* her now?"

"Do you not?" I say, lifting my eyes to his dark face. "Do you forget so quickly?"

"I do not forget," he says, "but that old fancy is dead and buried, thank God!" he throws out his arms with a gesture of freedom, "and is as little likely to be revived again as a body that has lain in the earth until it has fallen into dust."

"And she?" I ask, involuntarily.

"Has forgotten," he says; "why should she remember me? In fact, she seems positively to dislike me; never looks at or notices me, and I don't think we have exchanged twenty words."

"Yes," I say to myself, "and that is what makes me so sure. If she ever looked at or talked to you as to any one else——" But in him love is surely, certainly dead, for jealousy is the very pith and marrow of the passion, and he does not feel a single twinge.

"She does not care for him!" I say stoutly. "I have seen *real* lovers often: they are different. These are sham ones; to watch them is like looking at make-believe feasts, like we used to have at home."

Paul is loyal even to his buried love. He does not say, "She is coquette to the heart's core; she can never really care for any one." And I honour him as he holds his peace and says nothing.

It is a glorious afternoon. The hum of insects and birds is all about us; the ripe earth seems to hold the year's full perfection in her lap, like a gold flower that is wrought to its uttermost beauty. All too soon, alas! will it tremble and fade and wither away, for does not decay tread ever on the heels of all absolutely fair and lovely things? It is the common, ugly, every-day belongings that are never taken from us.

"And to-morrow this time," I say, as we turn back towards the house, following the gracefully interwoven forms of my sister and brother-in-law, "you will be perfectly happy among the birds! I wonder if any instinct tells them that this is their last day on earth?"

"It is to be hoped not! And what will you be doing?"

"Oh, I am going to enjoy myself too," I say brightly; "I shall have a long gossip with my sisters in the morning, and in the afternoon I shall go down by the sea."

"And take a book?"

"No. I have such heaps to think about!"

"People?"

"Plenty!—Mother, and Jack, and Dolly, and—and others."

"And others?" he repeats, bending his head to look into my face. "Tell me, among these others is there—a *Lubin?*"

CHAPTER VI.

"In the indications of female poverty there can be no disguise. No woman dresses below herself from caprice."

AT Luttrell our letters are brought up to us with our cup of early tea. Wise men tell us that our inveterate habit of tea drinking is in reality but another form of dram drinking, and that we are hardly less to be blamed than the poor gin-soddened wretches who reel hither and thither in our streets, a blot and a shame upon our country's manhood. They love their strong, coarse, deadly cups, and fly to them over ruined homes and women's broken hearts, and their own lost souls; and we who love our delicate, piquant, refreshing cup of tea, fly to it also, and reap our reward in shattered nerves and a hundred and one of the intangible, irritable disorders that our grandmothers and great-grandmothers never knew, or so many of them had not lived to such a full and healthy old age. It is a habit of self-indulgence, no doubt; and, perhaps, if the liquid really intoxicated us, we should have a tough battle with our inclination and give it up. Fortunately, however, it does nothing of the sort.

I have only one letter, and it lies on the tray, staring me in the face. Letters! What a little word, and what a lot it means! Only a flimsy bit of paper to guard secrets that might set the whole world agog; only a few beaten-out rags between prying, jealous eyes and the written down confirmation that, blared abroad, would carry wreck and ruin to many a proud and unblemished home.

Milord, reading his letters with a covert smile, on one side of the shallow breakfast table, glances over to where miladi sits, reading hers, with a curious expression flitting over her features. Neither knows any more than the dead who are each other's correspondents; but if each were to make a snatch across the table and exchange notes, perhaps husband and wife would get a better idea of the real character, aims, and life of the other than they ever had before. I like this Luttrell fashion of receiving and reading one's letters alone. It must be trying to have your neighbour watching your crestfallen countenance over unpleasant news, or your satisfied smile if you receive good. The face will sometimes expound the letter as clearly as though the writing were laid before the looker on.

And now for George's epistle. I have heard that love words written down are even sweeter than love words spoken; if it be so, must not unwelcome love-making be even nastier on paper than when spoken? I break the seal and take out the sheet, which is written over in a bold bright handwriting, very like his own looks. It is not very long or particularly eloquent, but it is manly and lover-like, and not sufficiently spoony, thank heaven, to read ridiculously. I think a good long course of such letters as these would impress me very favourably as regards him. If he only would be made to understand how much better I like him when he is sensible, than when he is talking nonsense! A man should be firm, yet tender; strong to govern, yet easily led. A woman despises him when he grovels abjectly at her feet; but he chills her when he soars away into the clouds. I wonder if I shall ever have a lover who will hit the happy mean?

This first of September has come upon us in kingly state, with mantle of azure and broad level sunbeams, with soft wooing breath and dew-spangled grass and leaf, and as I lean out of my window in the still early freshness of the morning, and look abroad at the beauty of hill and valley, land and sea, I marvel to myself whether the pretty brown birds are up and about, preening themselves in the sunshine, tasting of the gleaming dew, as happy and careless and ignorant to-day as they have been all through their short, merry, pleasant young lives.

Breakfast is early this morning, to suit the sportsmen, and when I go downstairs I find it well begun. The men are eating

with a healthy vigour that nothing short
of some prospective slaughter of bird or
beast ever inspires in their manly breasts.
They all look intensely awake, and upon
their countenances is that satisfied, all-is-
well expression that nothing on earth, save
the first of September, ever brings there.
Shorn of their nether garments, and clad
in knickerbockers, they stand confessed—
stalwart men of flesh and muscle, or weakly
miserable creatures, whose legs look as
though a touch would break them. Fane,
Charles Lovelace, Sir George Vestris, and
Paul Vasher · stand the test well; but the
others—ah, what a falling off was there!

The conversation is not particularly interesting; it is of "covers" and "coveys,"
"bags" and "beats," with many other
phrases that convey small meaning to our
ears, and once there is an indistinct murmur
of "luncheon and ladies." Yes, ladies
come last of all! For this is that day of
days when women, with a certain sinking
of the heart, or a sore smarting of their
vanity, are forced to confess that they
possess but a divided empire over the hearts

of men, and that fairer than all the charms
of his mistress, yea, sweeter even than the
breath of her lips and the music of her voice,
is to a man on this day the stubble under his
feet, the feel of a gun in his hand, and the
sight of a flock of little, soft, plump brown
birds. The knowledge is degrading, and we
all have a more or less hang-dog, neglected
air. Alice looks as though she were going
shooting too in her deft, workmanlike
Norfolk suit of grey. I wonder if, in the
city of veiled women in Siam, shooting is
practised by the gentler sex, as well as the
calling of policeman, soldier, and black-
smith?

Breakfast is over, and we are all leaving
the dining-room.

"Won't you wish me good luck?" asks
Paul Vasher, standing before me, big and
masterful in his cool grey clothes. (What
splendid legs he has got!)

"No, for you're bound on a bad errand.
On the contrary, I hope you will miss everything, and that "—I cast about flounderingly
for a suitable sporting phrase—"that your
neighbour will *wipe your eye!*"

He laughs. "Who taught you that expression?"

"I forget. Jack, I think. It was quite right, was it not?"

"Quite."

We are at the hall door now, where are gathered together sportsmen, keepers, and dogs, and a handful of young wives and maids. Milly is bidding her lord farewell for a whole day, with a fervour that many a death-bed parting lacks; Alice is standing on tiptoe to kiss Charles. It is as pretty a picture to my mind as any of Mr. Frith's.

"I hope," says Paul Vasher, "that you will enjoy your afternoon by the sea, and—— You never answered my question yesterday —was it an impertinent one?"

"It was," I say, looking at him steadily through the burning red of my cheeks. "What if I had asked you if you had a Dulcinea?"

"What, indeed!" he says, looking down on me with an amused laughter in his eyes.

"Are you coming, Vasher?" calls Fane; and he goes with the rest.

The girls they leave behind them stand at the door and look after them, and, when the last pair of legs has vanished, turn and look at one another with somewhat lack-lustre eyes. Eight women left to each other's society for a whole day! Well may we look dull. I want to get Alice and Milly to myself for a bit, but how about these others? Silvia speaks first. No fear of *her* putting up with a morning with her own sex. She is going to write letters in her room, she says, if Mrs. Luttrell does not mind. Mrs. Luttrell does not mind, and she goes away. The Listers are going to spend the morning in the garden, if Mrs. Luttrell pleases, so *they* vanish like-wise. Mesdames Fleming and Lister are still in bed, their morning toilettes being affairs of some importance, so we are free of all encumbrances and able to follow our own devices. Having worshipped the babies on our knees for a full hour, we go into Milly's boudoir.

"Only to think," I say, executing a *pirouette* on the tips of my toes, "that we three should be all together again here, and that there is no one to send us to bed, or call us names, or insist on our *talking !*"

"Is he as bad as ever?" asks Milly.

"He is worse!" I say with conviction. "When a person has got into a habit of making himself and everybody round him miserable, he does not stand still—he goes on improving. By the time he is sixty I cannot imagine what he will be!"

"Marry!" says Alice, encouragingly; "that is the only thing a spinster can do in self-defence!"

"You have been so lucky!" I say; "but how do you know I shall be the same? Besides, where is the husband to come from?" I add, laughing.

"But you have a lover," says Alice, "only you will not tell me anything about him."

"There cannot be much to tell yet, I should think," says Milly, with some sisterly rebuke in her tone. "Why, she has only known him since the day before yesterday!"

"Who are you talking about?" asks Alice, looking puzzled. "Nell's lover is not here at all; he is at Silverbridge."

"Is he not?" says Milly, with a queer smile. "I suppose I was mistaken."

"How refreshing it is to see any one blush," says Alice, meditatively. "Now in London, or good society, you never see the ghost of a blush anywhere!"

"But this Silverbridge lover," says Milly, with interest, "who is he—what is he—where did he come from?"

"He is a travelling packman," I say gravely. "I met him in the fields, and he came from Glasgow. We won't talk about him. Tell me, Milly, do you think that while I am here you will have a ball?"

"Tell me about this young man first," says Milly, "and I will tell you about the ball afterwards."

This is what I have been dreading; a long, comfortable, married women's conversation over my matrimonial prospects, with a calm and dispassionate balancing of *pros* and *cons*, in which my own heart will have no concern. For of all the strenuous advocates of two people marrying who are not particularly fitted for each other, commend me to a couple of young women who

have married for love and are perfectly
happy; they do not know what uncongenial
wedlock means, and cannot be brought to
understand its misery. I give a deep groan.
With these inquisitors I know of no arts that
will avail me save flight, and I do not wish
to run away; for, judging by an intangible
something in Milly's face just now, I have
a shrewd suspicion that not only is there
a ball, but that the day is fixed—so here
goes.

"Alice, Milly, I won't deny it. I have
got a lover, and his name is Tempest, and
he lives at Silverbridge, and I don't mean to
marry him if I can possibly help it; and I
have told him so, and he is very good-looking, and—and that's all!" Here I stop,
out of breath.

"Tempest!" says Milly; "I am sure I
heard Fane talking about some Tempests
the other day. Are they not very rich
people?"

"I believe so!"

"And why on earth don't you marry
him?" asks Alice, warmly. "You will see
nobody in Silverbridge; and as to living at

home with papa—— By the way, what does he say to your having a lover?"

"He does not know it, or at least he never says anything."

"Although it is all going on under his very nose!" says Milly. "Well, one of these days he will open his eyes very wide and be furious, and you will be sent to bed for a week."

"I expect he will make a great fuss," I say cheerfully. "I only hope he will lock me up altogether, for then George Tempest will not be able to get at me."

"Nell," says Alice, with a serious disbelief in her voice, "have you kept back anything?"

"What, about Mr. Tempest?"

"Of course. Now, you said he was good-looking—is he short?"

"He is over six feet."

"And he has not a hump?"

"No."

"Does he talk through his nose?"

"No."

"Or wear large plaid suits?"

"No."

"Is he ignorant? Not that that signifies, for nowadays only the middle classes are well informed; well-born people are nearly always doubtful as to their spelling."

"No," I say again.

"Is there insanity in the family," asks Milly.

"No! No! No!" I say, jumping up and going off into immoderate laughter. "He is nice, charming, desirable in every way; but— is it so very hard to understand?—I can't marry him, for I do not love him!"

"Then you are in love too with somebody else!" says Alice, scanning with broad-eyed candour my disturbed face, "though where you can have seen him I'm sure it is difficult to imagine."

"I am not in love!" I say indignantly; "I never was in love! I would not do anything so silly, so—so ridiculous. If I had had any fancy that way I should have made a donkey of myself at Silverbridge long ago."

"And how long have you been sure that you do not care about Mr. Tempest? Since the day before yesterday?" asks Milly, saucy persistence in her blue eyes.

"I have known it all along," I say steadily. "What should the day before yesterday have to do with it?"

"Nothing," says Milly, with a baffling glance at Alice. However, I will not notice their looks.

"And now for the ball," I say, fanning my heated countenance with the tail of my pannier. "Are you really going to have one?"

"On the 17th. Shall I send Mr. Tempest an invitation?"

"How delightful!" I say, drawing a deep breath. "I have never been to a dance in my life, you know, and——"

"What are you going to wear?" asks Alice, and her literal question brings me very suddenly down from the rose-coloured clouds on which I am floating. My jaw drops, and I stare at her blankly.

"I never thought of that," I say slowly; "I was thinking of the dancing and the fun, and——"

"Have you not a single ball dress?" asks Milly, rather cruelly I think, for she knows as well as I do how the governor mulcts us in pin-money.

"A ball dress!" I repeat, derisively. "Indeed, you may thank your stars that I have come in a gown at all, and not a petticoat body, for there is so much trouble to get any clothes at Silverbridge, that very soon, I believe, we shall have to do with none at all."

"Of course you must have a dress," says Milly, calmly; "had you not better write to Howell and James, and order one?"

Howell and James! When even that refuge of the destitute, William Whiteley, is far, far beyond me! Clearly Milly has forgotten the days of her youth.

"I shall not appear," I say miserably; "I could not dance and enjoy myself with an awful bill hanging over me all the evening, and knowing what it would cost mother, so I shall be *ill* the night of the party, unless you think a costume *à la* squaw, consisting of a pearl necklace and a pair of boots, would be full dress enough."

"It would be quite full enough," says Alice, "and extremely well suited to the weather, only Mrs. Grundy might object."

"If you had only been at Silverbridge at

the last bill row," I say, sinking into still deeper dejection, " you would not feel inclined to *laugh* at the prospect of another."

" Tell us about it," says my lovely sister; " those rows were terrifying things, but very amusing to think of after."

" The last *was* amusing," I say, laughing heartily, in spite of the dismal business of getting a gown that unpleasantly pervades my mind ; " you remember Snooks, the draper ? "

" Rather."

" You know the consternation his modest handwriting ever caused in our domestic circle ? Well, at midsummer he sent in his account, and of course papa, instead of paying it, danced upon it as usual. I fancy he has a notion that after dancing a *pas seul* over bills they are, in fact, discharged, don't you ? Well, times being bad with Snooks, he plucked up a spirit, and wrote a gentle request for his dues, but when it arrived no one could be found brave enough to present it to the governor; for two days it was handed round the house, everybody, servants and all, repudiating it, and then with one consent it was decided that something must be done. The Bull of Basan proposed that we should lay it on the Prayer-book, and receive in a body his overflowing wrath, but, after some consideration, that plan was rejected. Finally it was decided that we should place it in that little study at the top of the stairs, by his bed-room, where he often sits, and the time for putting it there was fixed at immediately after dinner, when he is always sitting in the library over his wine. Dinner over, Basan fetched the fatal epistle, and we set off, full speed, for the study, clattering up the stairs like mad, he first, I following. You know how narrow the staircase is, and that the door opens abruptly to the left, so that until you are right on to the threshold you cannot see in at all; well, Basan flung the door open and—stopped short: Alice! Milly! over his face came the most awful, indescribable, wonderful change; he looked as if he was turned to stone. Nothing short of the governor could produce that look on any of our faces, and *he* was down in the library.

"'What on earth is the matter?' I said, poking my grinning countenance round the corner; 'you look as if you had seen the dev—' There, within half a yard of my nose, stood *the governor!* The old gentleman would have been an agreeable apparition compared with that. Do you know the grin absolutely *froze* on my face; for a moment I stared, then turned tail and ran, Basan after me. Half-way down the stairs I remembered the bill.

"'You must go back and give it him!' I said in an agony, and I pushed him back.

" Meanwhile papa was capering at the top of the stairs in a perfect fury, asking how we dared go to his room, what we wanted there, did we mean to break the staircase in with our confounded boots, etc. When Basan went back with the letter, he tore it out of his hand, saw what it was, and then threw it at him! Basan never stopped to pick it up that time, he ran in good earnest, so did I! To this day it is a mystery to us how he got up there, for we *saw* him go into the library."

"I know it all so well," says Alice, drying

her eyes, " but we have had more amusing rows than that."

" Do you remember——" And here we slide off into a crowd of ludicrous reminiscences, that are very real and true, and ridiculous to us, but maybe would seem sad and unlikely enough to other people; perhaps they would not understand how we could laugh at all over such things, but, thank God, we have ever been able to find a silver lining to our clouds, and it is better to bear our ills with a smiling countenance, is it not, than to turn bitter, and hard, and cynical, and rail against heaven?

CHAPTER VII.

"The best of rest is sleep,
And that thou oft provok'st ; yet grossly fear'st
Thy death, which is no more."

WE are feeding the gold and silver fish in the pool before the drawing-room windows, Paul Vasher and I. He is providing for the silver ones, I for the gold, or at least am trying to, for the former, if they have duller backs, have far brighter wits than their orange-coloured brethren, and get the crumbs oftenest. "Do you know," I say, as I drop my last bit deftly into the greedy maw for which it was intended, "that we are going to have something most charming and delightful?"

"And what is that?" he asks, as we pace along the terrace side by side.

"A ball!" I say, clapping my hands; "a

real one, no make-believes this time! Will you ever forget that party at Charteris?"

As the words leave my lips, he looks across at Silvia, who is for a wonder sitting alone hard by, seemingly watching us with a listless indifference.

"I shall never forget that party," he says quietly; "and so you like the prospect of this ball?"

"Yes, indeed. Will you believe that I have never had a real partner in my life but once, and that was when I danced with you?"

"Have you not? Then for the sake of that old dance, you will give me the first, will you not?"

"Yes, but you must not be angry if I bungle dreadfully; I never could dance well!"

"Then why are you so pleased at the prospect of this party?"

"I shall like the music, and the fun, and my partners, and all that."

"And I suppose you are full of delight at having to choose a new gown and wreath!"

"Full of delight!" I stare at him blankly for a moment, then look away; he little knows what a gnashing of teeth business having a new gown in our family is. "It is not much of a pleasure," I say, with an odd smile; "it is far more of a misfortune."

"You are afraid of its not being becoming?" says Paul, looking puzzled; "have you decided on what it is to be?"

"I have not thought much about it yet: anything."

"Wear white," he says, with a man's fixed belief in the perfectibility of that colourless colour; black or white, or black *and* white, every man believes a woman to be well dressed when she is arrayed from top to toe in either, or both. Men have no notion of the innumerable little details that go to make up a perfectly appointed toilet; they will say that a woman looks well or ill, but they can't pick her to pieces, and tell you in what part of her dress the fault lies. They will pronounce one of Worth's choicest confections to be "hideous," and a simply but gracefully attired girl to be "charming;" having no feminine admiration—the barbarians!—for the costly lace and exquisite trimmings that mark the former, while the charming creature, poor soul! wears only ordinary muslin and ordinary silk.

"There are so many whites," I say, considering: "white silk, white satin, white brocade, white muslin—the materials are endless."

"And what had you on that day I met you among the rye?"

"A white cambric," I answer; adding mentally, "or a 'clean boiled rag,' as Jack calls it, and which the washerwoman knows as well as her own face!"

"If I tell you what to wear," says Mr. Vasher, "will you promise to have it?"

"So long as you do not put me in pink or yellow."

"Then you shall wear white of some glistening light fabric; and on one side you must have great bunches of gold wheat and scarlet poppies, with a little bunch of the same against your left shoulder, and a wreath in your hair."

"Not in my hair, please, Mr. Vasher! It is not so very long ago that it was almost red, and——"

"I don't think you need be afraid of the poppies," he says, looking at my untidy ruffled locks; "they looked well enough the other day."

"I only wore that wreath across the field out of sheer bravado," I say laughing, "because I had been told not to."

"Who told you not to?" he asks quickly; "who had the right to?"

"No one!" I say, turning my head away; "at least, no one in particular."

We walk in silence up the little steep path that leads towards the upper terraces. In front of us are Mrs. Fleming and Mr. Silvestre; following behind, Alice and Lord St. John: the men have returned from shooting early to-day. I am wondering what my dress will cost, and whether boughten poppies are expensive, also whether they are as handsome as their living sisters. After all I think I shall take Milly's advice. Papa could not possibly storm more over a big bill than he would over a little one, and, let the cost be what it may, I am resolved that on the 17th I will for once in my life be not merely clothed but *dressed!*

"I have made up my mind," I say, briskly, "my gown shall be made of white *gauze.* It ought to be beautiful, ought it not?"

"Very."

He is not looking at me but straight before him, and there is a thwarted, vexed look in his face.

"Are you cross?" I ask. "Are you thinking how frivolous and senseless I am to be thinking so much about my first ball?"

"No, child! I was wondering if it were possible for one to meet with a girl who had never——"

"Never what?"

"Nothing."

A silence falls between us as we pace along the gravel walks, the coolness of the late afternoon all about us, the greenness of the earth at our feet, God's azure carpet hanging royally over our heads; only the faint pure smell of an occasional wild flower comes to us on the air, for we are high up on the cliff now, and the gay garden flowers are too proud or too lazy to climb so high.

"And how soon will you be going back to Silverbridge?" asks Paul, his voice disturbing me in the midst of an agonizing calculation of how many yards of stuff an orthodox ample ball dress requires.

"Not until the end of the month." (Thirty, I should think. I wonder what gauze is a yard?)

"I suppose you are in a great hurry to get back?"

"Not at all! why should I be? Jack is in town, Dolly at school; it is very dull at home just now. And I have not been here ten days yet."

"But you have other friends in Silverbridge; there are some residents, are there not?"

"One or two." (I must have a pair of white satin shoes at Marshall's, and long gloves with a great many buttons—I shall not stick at a button or two.)

"Tell me their names, for they will be my neighbours too very shortly?'

"We have neighbours, but do not visit them, nor they us. Papa does not like them. We know only one family, and their name is—Tempest," I say, turning aside to pluck a modest spray of euphrasy, and looking down on its purple-streaked petals.

"A large family?"

"No; only a father and son."

Whether it is that I have really forgotten all about my absent lover, or that the thought of my new gown absorbs my faculties to such an extent that I am unable to entertain any other ideas, I do not, I am proud to say, blush in the very least, and am able to meet Paul's searching eyes without a ray of embarrassment or self-consciousness.

"And I suppose that it was because you had seen so few people that you recognized me when we met in the field of rye?"

"Perhaps. I had never known but two men in all my life—young men I mean—until I came here, so I could not very well forget, could I?"

"And I am very glad of it!" he says heartily.

"Are you? I am not! I do not think one is able to judge of whether a man is admirable or the reverse until one has seen a great many?"

"Women ought not to see too many men," he says decidedly, "it is bad for them." Paul Vasher is like the rest of his sex, who value their privileges too highly to permit women to encroach the merest jot upon them, and would build so prickly a wall of propriety around us, that we shall not even be able to climb up and see what is going on on the other side.

"That is very hard upon us," I say. "Is it not the author of 'Guy Livingstone' who says, that 'a man must see and admire many roses before he plucks the fairest of them all, his Provence rose, to lay in his breast?' You are free to walk about, looking at this flower and that, critically surveying all, able to make your choice after mature deliberation, while we may not look around us or seek to judge for ourselves; on the contrary, we must accept the first flower that is offered to us, think it adorable, perfect, fall down before it in worship, and look at it contentedly to the end of our days!" Here I stop, somewhat out of breath and laughing.

"Is she always bound to take the first?" he asks, looking at me very keenly.

"Almost always," I say, with a heavy sigh. "Must it not be hard when some day, and all too late, a woman who has given away her life like that, ignorantly, meets with some other who would have suited her? Ah! what ugly words those are, 'too late!' They always make me think of Balzac and the dream that ran through his toiling, barren life; of the tender woman's hands that should one day smooth the hair back from his weary brow, and say, 'Poor soul, thou hast suffered!' They came to him at last, too late."

"Do you know," says Paul, "that you have the saddest face sometimes, child, that I ever saw?"

"Do I look like a girl who is going to have a miserable story?" I ask, stopping short; "do I look like a girl who is going to die young?"

He takes my two hands in his, and looks

down with infinite gentleness on my pale, scared face.

"God forbid!" he says gently.

"Do not think me a very great coward; do not despise me," I say, shivering; "but I so fear death. I have such a bodily horror and shrinking away from it, not for what it brings, but because I so dread to go away, to be caught out of this warm, beautiful earth that I know, and away from all the people and things I love. I enjoy my life so keenly that I could not bear to let it go. Do you think I shall be punished? Is it impious to feel like this?"

"You sweet little soul!" he says, in his strong, tender voice, "you be punished for aught in your fair young life? I wonder what God would reserve for sinners such as I, then?"

"You are not a sinner," I say stoutly, looking into his noble face — a face that gives so much more promise of grand things than he has ever worked in his life yet. "You are *good*."

I loose my hands from his, and we walk on again side by side.

"Do you know," I say laughing (Why does laughter often follow so quickly on the heels of sighs?), "that if I know you long I shall become the most egotistical, maundering little person in Christendom? You listen to my complainings, at home no one ever does! Who was it said that there were two people in the world one should never trust one's self to talk about—one's self and one's enemy?"

"A foolish man whoever he was," says Paul, "who knew nothing of human nature, for are not those two naturally the most interesting people under the sun?"

"I do not think I have an enemy?" I say, considering; "have you?"

"No particular one that I know of, though there are plenty of people who dislike me, no doubt. When you are back at Silver-bridge, Nell, I shall see you very often, shall I not?"

"If papa does not take a dislike to you."

"I shall be glad to be back there," he says, with a hearty content in his voice. "After a bit, I suppose, I shall settle down and grow fat!"

" I don't think so," I said, glancing at his clean length of limb. " A man need never do that unless he pleases; he has so many active exercises by which he can ward off stoutness. Now, a woman has only got to sit down, and be free from worry of body or soul, to grow fat directly ! "

" Then some day I may expect to see you of very comely proportions ? "

" No, lean and haggard and ill-favoured very likely, but stout never. I bother myself too much over everything for that."

" Your husband will take better care of you," he says; then, bending his head to look into my eyes with those splendid dark ones, that send so sharp and quick a pain through my heart, " has it never occurred to you, child, that some day you will marry ? "

" Everybody marries at some time or another, do they not? It is a solid heavy pudding of which all taste in turn ! "

" Except the old maids ? "

" I had forgotten them, but they have probably had lovers in their time; and after all, the courting must be so much pleasanter than the hard and fast wedlock!"

"I think your experience of married people cannot have been very fortunate," says Paul, looking amused. "Why should not people love each other after they are married as well as before?"

"They ought, but very often they do not! They begin very hot and end very cold; and I was wondering only yesterday whether, if one married somebody one did not care about, one would gradually get *warmer* towards him?"

"It would be rather a dangerous experiment," says Paul; "were you thinking of trying it?"

I do not answer, and as at this moment we fall in with Fane and Milly, he has no opportunity of repeating his question.

CHAPTER VIII.

ANGELO. Nay, women are frail too.
ISABELLA. Ay, as the glasses where they view themselves,
Which are as easy broke as they make forms.

IT is high noon, and we are "six precious
souls, and all agog," dashing along the
dusty, hot, turnpike road towards Beecham
Wood. The sun, knowing that his time is
short, and that he will ere long sink from
the proud overbearing tyrant into a mild,
benevolent, dull old luminary, is beating
down upon us with broad level strokes,
cleaving our parasols and tickling our faces,
making us, in short, very uncomfortable,
cross, and miserable. It is the sort of day
when one longs instinctively for an open
unoccupied space, no living being near
to touch one, and nothing to do save im-
bibe cooling drinks; therefore pity us, oh

reader! in that I am shut up with three other females in Milly's landau. Behind us follows a carriage similarly filled, and we are *en route* for the vernal shades of Beecham and the society of the sportsmen, with whom we are going for the first time to take luncheon. They have several times asked humbly enough for our society, but with the first lust of slaughter upon them Milly judged wisely that they were best left to their own and the birds' company. They are somewhat sated by now, though, for to-day is the 16th of the month.

How fast the days have slipped away! How utterly pleasant and sweet they have been! Let me not begin to rejoice over them though, lest evil ones follow. Far away I see a little soft cloud of grey under the trees, with dogs lying about. As we approach nearer it resolves itself into the gentlemen, who are lounging about, cigar in mouth, looking as cool, and fresh, and comfortable as we look precisely the reverse. We all tumble out of the carriages anyhow, and make a dash through the gate, only longing to get into the shady woodland beyond. In the general scrimmage Lord St. John is tossed up nearest to me.

"Have we much farther to go?" I ask, looking with affection at a big tree we are hurrying past.

"Not much!" he says; "two or three minutes' walk, perhaps."

I don't think he has done much shooting this morning: he looks as if he had come out of a bandbox, and his wicked little eyes are fixed with doting fondness on Alice's vanishing tail, for with all my haste I am somehow the very last of all.

Everybody seems to have got badly matched to-day: Alice is with Captain Brabazon, Milly with Mr. Silvestre; Fane's back expresses intense disgust as he walks by the side of Mrs. Lister, and her daughter's head has a sulky air as seen in the company of Charles Lovelace, while—oh, wonder of wonders—Silvia Fleming has fallen to the lot of Paul Vasher, and Sir George Vestris gloomily stalks with that young woman's mother.

I am casting my eyes about the wood, and thinking how pretty it is now, and how

infinitely prettier it must be in spring-
time, thickly powdered over with dainty
forest flowers, when I put my foot into a
rabbit hole and take a breathless header
into space. Lord St. John picks me up
without a smile, likewise my hat, which has
ambitiously flown far beyond my head, like
a rider who clears a fence while his horse
remains behind. Goëthe says men show
their character in nothing more clearly than
in what they think laughable. Now Lord
St. John does not even smile, whereas if I
had seen him meet with the same accident
I should have laughed immoderately for
five minutes. There is no one behind to
mark my confusion, so, as one's misfortunes
are always bearable when there is no one by
to observe them, I put on my hat with
unruffled serenity and proceed on my way.

What a dull little lord this is! It is
lucky that he does not, like other mortals,
depend on "the quantity of sense, wit, or
good manners he brings into society for the
reception he meets with in it." He is
neither handsome, nor wise, nor witty, yet
he will never know the lack of good looks,

wisdom, or sense; he will pass over the
heads of men better in every way than himself, only they are born with wooden ladles
in their mouths, and he with a silver one.

Here we are at last! The white cloth
on the grass, commends itself favourably
to my eyes, and the twinkling silken calves
of the footmen, as they go hither and
thither, look festive and cool. I sit down
with a sigh of relief, and Paul Vasher comes
to my side and sits down too. Sir George
flies to Silvia, Milly to Fane; the sisters,
alas! to the Captains—it is a general post.
I wonder what Paul and Silvia have been
talking about: there is no expression on her
face; on his there is a great deal, as he
looks at me. I have hardly dared to seek to
learn its meaning yet—hardly ventured to
put out a trembling hand to touch the skirt
of a mantle of great joy.

Everybody is sitting down now, and finding by painful experience that though
eating one's luncheon on the grass is a
picturesque thing to look at, it is by no
means a comfortable thing to do: one's
back has an awkward trick of curving out-

wards, and one's knees of encroaching on one's chin. Then the eating—whether is it better to bend two double over the plate on the damask, or permit it to reverse itself and its contents on our slippery laps? In spite of these drawbacks, however, the grateful shadow, gay voices, welcome champagne cup, and the right companion, make the hour a pleasant one. If only these pleasant hours that come so rarely to us mortals would abide with us, not hurry so fleetly away!

"I think you must have snubbed St. John pretty well," says Paul; "he left you so precipitately just now."

"He is so stupid," I say, looking across at him; "and as I am not clever myself I like to be with amusing people: do not you?"

"Indeed, I do: but I don't think the cleverest people are the most amusing. They go too deep. It is the nonsense talkers who are most companionable; just as you will laugh heartily at a book that you keep on saying to yourself over and over again is the silliest stuff imaginable."

"Then there is some hope for me, is there not?"

The servants come and go, merry jests are born and die, the sunbeams flicker jubilantly down on our uncovered heads, the butterflies flutter idly by, the gnats swarm above us, there is a sleepiness in the air, a sense of comfort in our bodies.

"What have you been thinking about all this time?" asks Paul.

"You will laugh if I tell you," I say, "but just then I was ruminating about bread sauce. Partridges grew and so did bread, but the man who wedded the two must have been a clever fellow, must he not?"

"And you were really thinking that?"

"Really! I suppose it was the sight of the birds yonder put it into my head."

He looks at me amusedly.

"I wonder if you could keep a secret if you had one?" he says. "I think you would bring it straight out. I always know when you are glad or sorry, vexed or pleased, in an instant; do you think you could be deceitful if you tried?"

"You don't know what stories I can tell

at a pinch," I say, laughing; " and if that is not being deceitful, what is ? "

" You do not mean that you tell *lies ?* "

" What a downright word! How ugly it makes the smallest deviation from truth look! No, my fibs are only harmless ones, extemporized to save the boys from getting into rows with papa, and so forth. I don't ever remember telling a real lie."

"And you have never deceived *anybody?*" he asks, with a strange persistence.

" Never! " I say, truly—for have I not told George the plain unvarnished truth hundreds and hundreds of times ?

Luncheon is over, and most of the men are not sitting but lounging at their ease, with a comfort very irritating to feminine eyes. Alice and Milly are making use of their respective lords by leaning against them *dos-à-dos ;* the attitude is comfortable but not particularly elegant. A score of yards away a stalwart oak presents to our view a stout brown body that offers friendly support to an aching back, and towards it I turn my eyes.

"You are tired," says Paul; "shall we go and sit over there?"

He holds out his hand, pulls me up, and in another minute we are sitting against the old monarch.

"How tired that lord must have got who went on a tour round England without once leaning back in his carriage!" I say laughing. "Don't you think he must have taken it out in a long course of easy chairs afterwards?"

"I don't fancy they had any worth mentioning in those days. What hardy old people they were, and to what an age they lived! Now-a-days it is the old who bury the young. I think it was their leisurely way of taking things, their conversations, their journeys, their love-makings, that kept their bodies and souls so fresh. They were content to take life gradually: one emotion at a time was enough for them; they knew how to wait. Our generation is not satisfied with looking forward; it must desire, long for, possess, all in a breath. There is very little patience anywhere in this nineteenth century."

"I should have liked to live in those days," I say, thinking; "they lived such much grander, sweeter, honester lives than we do: they must have had so much more of eternity, so much less of the present, in their thoughts than we have!"

"Let me tell you, child," says Paul, "that there are girls in the world every bit as nice and honest and sweet as their grandmothers were. Do you remember," he asks, drawing nearer to me, "that once, years ago, I assured you it was much better to be good than pretty? And you disappointed me a good deal, by seeming to prefer the prettiness to the goodness!"

"It was not for beauty's sake I wished it," I say, looking ashamed; "but because I had always thought it a great power, and because I saw handsome people treated far more kindly than plain ones!"

"Do you not know, child, that far more deeply rooted in a man's breast than the mere admiration of physical beauty, is his veneration of what is pure, and not to be corrupted, something better than himself, in a word—good? Many women believe that they can hold an undivided empire over a lover's heart by being simply lovely to the eye, and charming : they trust to the comeliness of the body effectually preventing any search after the soul or mind, and their experience of a certain class of men justifies them in so believing. Of the far larger class, who put aside all the dazzle and beauty of the outside appearance to look beyond, they have no conception, little knowing that every sensible man, if he do admire the sparkling casket, always looks within to see if it contain a gem of value and purity, or a tawdry bit of coloured glass."

"You are very hard upon us," I say, surprised. "Are all men so difficult to please as you?"

"Shall I tell you why we see the faults of women so freely?" he says. "Because we know how infinitely above us most of you are in purity, unselfishness, and goodness, it is because we hate to see you step off your pedestals and come down to our level, that we are so severe upon every failing and shadow of evil doing. Do we not honour

you more in setting you a high standard,
than a low one?"

"But do you not help to lower it?" I
ask. "I have never been out into the world;
I have only read and heard people talk: but
I think, if girls are frivolous and vain, it is
you who help to make them so. If you
talked nobly and sensibly to them and tried
to bring out, not the amusing weakness of
their characters, but the hidden worth that
lies in every nature, you would make less of
toys, more of companions of them."

"You are right," he says; "men do in-
calculable harm in fostering the vanity
and conceit of girls; but it is a fact that
you may tell a woman she is virtuous,
discreet, admirable in every way, and she
will not say thank you; but tell her she
is pretty—and smiles will break out all
over her face. Fellows know this, and of
course take advantage of the weakness, and
so society becomes leavened with a general
idea that beauty is the greatest good and
blessing on earth, and that all the other
virtues and graces are set down second to
it. There never was a greater fallacy. Now,

if I had a wife, her good looks would be the last thing I should care to hear commented on. It would give me no pleasure to hear people exclaiming, 'How pretty she is!' 'How beautifully she dances!' but if they said, 'She is a thorough little lady,' 'She is sensible and charming,' 'She is good,' I should be proud of her, and in nothing so much as this, that no one would dare offer her the smallest liberty, in look or word."

"Are you reading me this homily on the beauty of goodness *versus* the goodness of beauty, to comfort my forlornness?" I ask laughing. "Indeed, you need not : I have grown quite used to not being pretty like the rest."

"Pretty," he says, staring at my face, "can you be so—— ?" He checks himself, and breaks off. "I see your brothers are smoking," he says presently, "may I ?"

"Yes."

I look around me. Mrs. Lister is fast asleep, propped up against a neighbouring tree. Her mouth is wide open, and the flies are walking in and out of the same as seemeth good to them. Her daughters are pursuing their up-hill, one-sided flirtations; and the head of the elder is wobbling plaintively towards Captain Brabazon's shrinking shoulder in a manner that seems to say, "let me lay it down, *and leave it.*" Mrs. Fleming is reading a letter, and her squire —Mr. Silvestre—lies on his back by her side, deeply, soundly, noisily asleep. Silvia is telling her fortune on a spike of grass, and looking with lovely, lazy eyes at Sir George, whose face is aflame with love, pleading, and God alone knows what. Fane's cheek rests contentedly on Milly's elaborate chignon; and Alice, leaning against Charles's broad back, listens to Lord St. John's mild conversation and flatteries with half-shut eyes. The content on Paul's face is good to behold, when he has his cigar fairly between his lips. Was ever woman, I wonder, as true and faithful and kind a friend to man as tobacco?

"Your sex ought to be better tempered than ours," I say; "for you are able to smoke away all your troubles and disappointments and annoyances, while we can only sit down and think."

"You have one great resource that is denied to us—you can weep."

"That is so cowardly. I always look upon tears as a refuge only to be fled to when everything else fails (I mean, of course, when I am put out), and of the two I would far rather storm."

"And yet," says Paul, "utterly as you can rout us by the sight of your tears, I prefer even them to being reviled by you —a woman's power is pretty well gone when she takes to scolding."

"Cleopatra kept hers well enough," I say, half to myself. "Now if I were you, I would far rather have a woman who was outrageous sometimes and sorry afterwards, than a meek, obstinate, crying creature who never forgot herself—or a grudge."

"Then you prefer Katherine to Bianca?"

"Infinitely; and I am certain I should have slapped Bianca even harder than Katherine did. She only insisted on her own way until she found some one with a stronger will, then she gave in directly."

"And would you give in to any one?"

"If I were quite sure his ways were

better than mine, if not I should take my own."

"You ought to take his whether you are sure or not."

"Indeed! I see the race of tyrants is not quite extinct."

"Or that of rebels!"

"There should be no question of 'giving in' or 'looking up,'" I say demurely. "Alfred de Musset says a woman should above all things be *bon camarade;* and between comrades there is equality, is there not?"

"The man should always rule," says Paul, in his masterful way; "and you may say what you like, Nell, but you would love to be ruled, you would like to be kept in order."

"No, no," I say gravely; "that Frenchman's idea was a much better one. He went on broader grounds than you do. Yours is an English notion. He recognized the fact that however pretty and amusing it may be to play at love, it cannot be made the business of a life-time; and that after a while a man grows tired of treating his mistress or wife like a goddess or a baby: he wants more solid stuff to live on, and the one everlasting dish palls then. If she will look the knowledge in the face that such is the case, and putting sentiment on one side enter heartily into his ambitions and aims, and hopes, and amusements, she becomes not only the beloved woman, but the bright pleasant comrade, who is bound to him by fifty ties of mutual interest and support; they are equals, and he considers her as capable of giving advice as taking it——"

I stop short in my serious disquisition on love and matrimony as I catch Paul's amused smile.

"Wait until you fall in love," he says; "I shall see it some day, and I wonder where all your philosophy will be then?"

"Where it is now," I answer stoutly, through my blushes, "nothing will ever alter my opinion on that point. I think it is nothing but bad management that makes so many married people who begin with so much love end up with so little. Mr. Vasher?"

" Yes ? "

" Do you think Silvia would ever have been *bon camarade?* "

" No, she would keep a man to her side by sheer fascination, but she could never—"

" What do you call fascination ? " I ask as he pauses.

" I suppose the real essence of it lies in the power a woman possesses of making herself so delightful, that every hour spent away from her is an age."

" Do witty people fascinate ? "

" In a different way. They amuse and astonish more than they inspire respect."

" How I should like to be witty ! " I say laughing. " It is a great power, is it not, to be able to say clever, brilliant, sparkling things ? "

" Yes, but one not often to be coveted. A very witty person is no one's enemy so much as his own : he amuses people at the expense of others, and the former have a pleasant conviction that their turn will come presently, and no one feels safe."

" Like Lady Hester Stanhope," I say, " who lost all her friends through her tongue, and was also known to boast that no one could give such a slap on the face as she could!"

"Yes, her wit worked her ruin," says Paul, "as did poor Brummel's, although indeed his was but barefaced effrontery!"

"I always admired that man," I say laughing: "he was so bold, and his insolence was so splendidly audacious. I wonder what master of ceremonies now-a-days would dare say to a duchess, 'In heaven's name, my dear duchess, what is the meaning of that extraordinary back of yours? I declare I must put you on a back-board. You must positively walk out of the room backwards that I mayn't see it!'" We both laugh heartily.

"It makes one feel very small, does it not," says Paul, "that people should feel so much more angry at being made fun of, than being called ugly, or wicked, or disagreeable? Is it not Macaulay who says, 'Alas for human nature, that the wounds of vanity should smart and bleed so much longer than the wounds of affliction!'"

"One can forgive unkindness, ill-usage,

neglect even—but ridicule never!" I say laughing; "and yet it is curious, is it not? to see how people like to make fools of themselves comfortably, but hate to be told of it. That, I suppose, is why you men always like to marry a stupid woman, who never finds you out!"

"You are wrong," says Paul. "A stupid woman, *i.e.* a fool, admires everything, and everybody, her husband among the rest; a sensible woman looks all about her, and seeing nothing half as good as the man she has married, admires *him*?"

"A most delicate flattery; but supposing he is not wise?"

"Would a woman of sense marry a man who had none?"

"She often does. Now Mrs. Skipworth at Silverbridge, she is sensible, and she married a very prosy, foolish man. And yet," I add, looking out at the cool green shadows and gold patches of sunlight that lie athwart the woodland, "I don't know that he is so foolish as irritating. Did you ever know a man who smiles when he tells you the day is fine, smiles when he tells you your soul is lost, and would smile over your new-made grave, and say the funeral had gone off beautifully? That is Mr. Skipworth!"

"Well," says Paul, "I shall see him before long, and listen to his sermons, which I suppose will be rather worse than himself. Is your seat in church anywhere near mine?"

"Oh no! The Towers turns up its nose at the Manor House, and while you rejoice in a curtained pew under the pulpit, we occupy an abased position in the aisle! The pew opposite yours was ours once, but it would not hold us all, and papa exchanged it for a big one; but there is scarcely any one to sit in it now—there are only nine of us altogether, babies and all!"

"Only nine!" he says. "Well, I shall come over to the Manor House often, and you will——"

"Nell, Nell!" cries Milly's voice in the distance, and I jump up hastily. Everybody has left off sleeping, talking, laughing, and flirting; the men are repossessing themselves of their guns, and the ladies are standing about.

"At any rate," says Paul, "we have stolen two pleasant hours from that old thief Time, have we not?"

CHAPTER IX.

"Through tattered clothes small vices do appear; robes and furr'd gowns hide all."

Nine o'clock is striking, and I am standing before a looking-glass, admiring myself with a hearty appreciation that it would be folly indeed to expect any one else to feel. For the first time in my life I am *en grande tenue*. With something of the recklessness of a man who decides that, if he must be hung, it may as well be for a sheep as a lamb, I am arrayed with a sublime disregard to such vulgar considerations as pounds, shillings, and pence, as might well set the governor dancing a *fandango* if he were but here to see; not but what he will dance it safely enough over the bill. Out of my glistening dress of gauze poppies burn redly, in great bunches at my side, and on my shoulder, and in my hair; they even twinkle cheerfully on my little white satin shoes, that look vastly pretty but pinch most horribly.

A tap at the door, and enter Milly's maid with a bouquet, "With Mr. Vasher's compliments." As she retires I take it in my hand. It is of blood red and yellow gold roses with a few ferns, and they look out of place with my vagrant wild flowers. I shall carry them though for all that. A supremely happy, well-dressed, blessed young woman I look as I take up my fan and gloves, and run lightly down the stairs.

My first ball! Will it be as disappointing, I wonder, as the fulfilment of most earthly wishes usually is? I make my way to the ball-room, wide and cool and lovely with the beauty of fair proportions, and delicate, brilliant dazzle of flowers.

The musicians are in their places, but nobody is visible, not even that mythical personage, the first arrival. Was ever any one known to confess that he or she arrived first anywhere? And yet somebody must, unless indeed several people race each other

to the hall door, and from the hall door to
the reception-room, and burst in on the
host and hostess simultaneously, like "three
jolly butcher boys all of a row." I have
laid down my bouquet, and am wrestling
with the fourth button of my long gloves (I
think I rather overdid them, they nearly
reach to my elbow), when Milly sails in,
majestic, gorgeous, with the value of the
clothes of twenty ordinarily well-dressed
females on her back.

"Good gracious!" she says, catching
sight of me, "how—how decent you look!"

"Yes," I say with delight, "is it not
wonderful? I had no idea so much virtue
lay in a gown!"

"Upon my word!" says Alice's gay voice
behind me. "Talk about the ugly duck-
ling——"

I turn round to look at her, a dainty
apparition in pale amber, with sapphires
twinkling on her arms, neck, and hair.
Alice is one of those fortunate people whom
each colour seems to suit better than the
last. Dress her in blue she is heavenly;
in pink she is ravishing; white sets her off

to perfection; and I have even known her emerge radiant from a bilious bottle-green serge that might have puzzled the fairness of Cytherea herself.

"Do not revive that stale, stale old story," I say entreatingly. "I know it is my clothes, not me; but let us try and shut our eyes to the fact. Let us for one evening indulge in the pious fiction that I am *good-looking!*"

"I don't know that it is altogether your dress," says Alice, considering. "I have seen you look astonishingly well once or twice lately. If I had not always been so used to the idea that you were plain, Nell, I should say you were rather pretty."

Much as I have been admiring myself, this unexpected praise makes me feel modest, and I turn the conversation with considerable haste.

"Has any one seen Silvia yet? I suppose she will be in something wonderful."

"Was Silvia Fleming ever known to waste her sweetness on the desert air?" asks Alice, seating herself. "When the company is assembled, and the music strikes up, she will appear, not before!"

"I do wish Fane would come down," says Milly, who is arranged in the expectant attitude of a hostess, on a high and ample crimson velvet chair, that to the vulgar eye bears a wonderful resemblance to a throne. "He always behaves in this way: it is too bad."

Like other women, Milly likes to be supported when she is receiving her guests; but Fane, doting lover and obedient spouse that he is, distinctly objects to the process of standing still and saying, "How do you do?" for an hour at a stretch, and when it is his plain and bounden duty so to do— makes himself scarce. Here come the Listers! Lister *mère* in a low (save the mark!) black velvet, with uncommonly fine diamonds resting on her withered, brown, fleshless old collar-bones, I suppose mahogany is a better foil to the precious stones than alabaster, since it is so much oftener seen. Her daughters wear apple-green silk and apple-blossom flowers, harrowing contrast! and the eye aches as it rests on the inharmonious whole. Will our matrons and maids ever, I wonder, learn to drape their garments, following the lines of the figure as a sallow Frenchwoman does, instead of breaking out all over in angles, tags, and excrescences?

A confused sound in the distance heralds an arrival.

"Nell," says Milly hastily, "will you find Fane, and make him come here at once?"

Rather a difficult matter that; I set out, however, with a bold front, and a regret that I have not been able after all to see the first people walk in. Ascending the stairs, I hear cackles and sounds of merriment above me. Looking up, I discover Fane and that other choice spirit, Captain Oliver, cutting capers on the landing, and evidently prepared to decamp at a moment's notice if any emissary from Milly appears upon the scene.

"Milly says——" I begin rebukingly.

"I know," says Fane, swinging me round to his side in a manner that may be indicative of brotherly affection, but certainly is not good for my gauze trappings.

"Now, Nell, did you ever see so much *back* as that before?"

Following his example, I crane my head and body over the banisters until I nearly precipitate myself into the hall below, and am rewarded by the sight of a dowager who looks as though her enemy had assaulted her from the rear, and robbed her of half her clothes.

"The older she gets," says Fane, "the more she shows; and the Lord only knows what further revelations Time may have in store for us!"

"She couldn't go much further," I said comfortingly. "I never knew before that middle-aged people's backs were of a rich *coffee* colour, did you, Fane? Who is that shambling little man?"

"Bareback's husband. She might wear him as a bustle and never know he was there."

The stream below widens, swells; people come pouring past in tens and twenties, sleek and clean and glossy, freshly powdered, freshly crimped, freshly smiling. What a pity that they will all be so draggled, and hot, and frowzy in two hours' time! Fat mammas, portly papas; pretty young girls, well preserved old ones; young boys, old boys, middle-aged boys; women white-backed, yellow-backed, brown-backed; women dressed by Elise, women dressed by themselves, well-groomed, ill-groomed, over-dressed, under-dressed, and not dressed at all. Truly it is a "motley crowd," and from our vantage ground we criticize them with the unripe sarcasm of our not over-wise youth.

I wonder why the young, and those who have only had the bright side of life turned to them, are so pitiless to the peculiarities, the faults, and the follies of others? It is only the old who are tolerant, and speak more kind words of their fellow-men than malicious ones.

After a quarter of an hour's impartial survey of the charms passing beneath us, "I think," says Fane, "I may venture down now without being let in by Milly for twenty-five duty dances."

Rum-tum-tum-tiddy! goes the music.

"Come along," cries Fane, "you and I will have the first together, Nell!"

"Miss Adair is engaged to me for this,"

says Paul's voice behind me. How long has he been there, I wonder? "I have been looking for you everywhere," he says, as Fane and Captain Oliver go downstairs. "I thought your toilette must have proved a wonderfully complicated affair."

"Do you like me?" I ask, stepping back from him, and holding out my skirts in my hands. "You chose it for me, you know; and, to tell you a secret, to-night I am not Helen Adair at all: I am *Howell & James!*"

"Like you?" he says, coming a pace nearer and looking at me keenly from head to foot, and from foot back to head again; "No, I don't *like* you!"

"I am so sorry," I say disappointedly. "I thought I looked so nice! I was so charmed with myself!"

"I like your poppies," he says, touching those upon my shoulder with the tip of his finger. "They make these things very well, do they not?"

"I will never ask you anything again as long as I live," I say, with dignity. "You might have tried, at any rate, to say something just a *little* polite;" and I march away.

But he catches my hand, flowers and all; and then I remember that I have not yet thanked him for his bouquet.

"Did I vex her," he says, looking down on my flushed face. "Was she such a vain little soul after all? Nell, Nell! after all the times I have exhorted you not to care about being pretty?"

"I am not vain," I say, turning my head away: "I never had anything to be vain of! But when one has been quite ugly for a very long while, and been told so every day of one's life, it is very disheartening, just as one begins to think one can look decent, for a person to say your dress looks nice, not you."

"There will be plenty of men to tell you that when you get downstairs, child," he says. "Can it make any difference to you what I think?"

"No, of course it does not!" I say magnanimously, and ashamed of my temporary fit of vanity. "I could not expect you to say what you did not think, could I?"

"If I were to tell you all I thought," he says, looking down on me, "I should frighten you, perhaps, and you would not understand. Perhaps you will let me tell you some day."

"Let us go down," I say, with a sudden shrinking away from him; "the first dance is already over."

Yes, it is over, and in the hall the people are pacing up and down, backwards and forwards, talking, laughing, flirting, in all the first gloss of their smartness; the men reduced to the smallest possible quantity of clothes, the women swelling forth in a lavish prodigality that mocks at "yards" and makes light of "breadths." Among them all I do not see any face I know; but a great many people nod and bow, and call acquaintance with Paul Vasher.

The haunting, matchless strains of "Blue Danube" come floating out to meet us as we enter the ball-room, and Paul puts his arm about my waist and we glide away, the first couple. After all it is not difficult to dance when one has a perfect partner: perhaps he adapts his step to mine—at any rate, we move in harmony. As the room becomes crowded we stop and sit down to look around us. Truly the scene is amusing enough, for everybody is revolving who has the means, without any question as to suitability in the age or size of that means: tall men dancing away from little partners, little men convulsively clutching tall women, old men and young maids, married women and young boys, fat girls dancing with Don Quixotes, Sancho Panzas puffing round with lean virgins. Everybody seems to have got the wrong partner, and not to mind it in the least. There are couples who rush round and round the room, crashing through every obstacle, and leaving overturned bodies, sore shins, and angry hearts behind ; leisurely couples who tread their measures delicately, and are invariably overtaken and run down by the more bustling couples who come behind; couples who aimlessly drift about and are knocked to and fro by the rest. . . .

"I never saw myself dancing," I say to Paul, "but do you think I ever looked like that ?" I glance at Miss Lister, whose head is wandering all over her partner's shirt front, seeking rest and finding none.

"I will look at you presently when you are dancing with somebody else, and tell you," he says.

"How well she dances!" I exclaim, nodding towards a mountain of fat that is going by, held together by a whipper-snapper whose arm refuses to go any farther than the last hook and eye. "Can you tell me why those enormous women go round so sweetly? They seem to turn on a pivot! What a pity it is this one does not live in a place I once heard of, where women are sold by the pound—flesh, not good looks, being considered the most marketable commodity!"

"Only she might object to being sold," says Paul, laughing. "Shall we go on again?"

"Look at St. John," says Paul, as we pause to take breath. "However earnest his solicitations, do not be prevailed upon to dance with him: he has a knack of making spectacles of his partners."

"But I have promised," I say, with some dismay. "He asked me at dinner, and of course I was obliged to say yes. Do you not know that anything in the shape of a partner is better than none at all?"

"You will know plenty of people presently," he says. "Don't believe all the nonsense they will talk to you, child."

"But I like nonsense: it is far more amusing than heavy common sense; besides, ball-room conversation is never expected to be very wise, is it?"

The music has ceased and we are walking down the room, past the wallflowers—prim and patient, with their white, white boots, that by-and-by will be their shame not their glory, and their sweet little smile that seems to say "We are sitting down, certainly; but only because we much prefer doing so to dancing!"—past the portly, coffee-backed observant dowagers, and so to Milly, who is looking with real indignation at Fane's rapidly vanishing heels, which he has been shaking with much agility ever since he came downstairs. She is talking to a long, lean, liver-coloured gentleman whose name I hear is Viscount Linley. We are all standing together when Silvia Fleming comes slowly past, the eye of every man and

woman present following her. She is all
white and crimson, and her fairness shows
more dazzlingly than ever against Sir George
Vestris' dark beauty.

"Are you not going to dance with Miss
Fleming to-night?" I ask, as we move
away. "If so, you had better be quick in
asking her, for in five minutes her card will
be full."

"Therefore I will not presume to ask so
great an honour," he says. "And now,
Nell, will you let me see your card?"

It is hanging at my side—an unmarked
expanse as spotless as the wallflowers'
boots; and I feel rather ashamed of it.

"You will keep all your waltzes for
me?" he says, scribbling down his initials
at somewhat short intervals.

"Yes; that is to say, if you do not
meet with somebody whose waltzing you
prefer to mine."

We walk about and make confidential
remarks to each other concerning the
company. We agree that those bare-
necked, plumed old dowagers are unpleasant
spectacles; but that the decorous, high-

gowned, middle-aged folk who wear their own hair, and not too many fal-lals, are good to look upon, and by no means to be pitied, since they have had their fun, danced their jigs, and now, youth's fits and fevers, ups and downs past, they cannot be sorry to sit down in their comfortable prosperity, and rest. We agree that it would be a kindness on the part of any one present to fetch a shawl to cover Mrs. Lister's unveiled charms; but on my suggesting that Paul should take a neighbouring antimacassar to her with his own compliments, he proves himself to be greater at discretion than valour. We think it would be a hard nut for a philosopher to crack if he were called on to decide why so many ancient, purblind, doting old people persist in going to balls, where they are neither useful nor ornamental, and are divided in opinion as to whether supper and scandal are the attractions, or an obstinate determination not to confess themselves too old for society and conviviality, is at the root of the matter. We decide that the lack of *tournure* in the girls present is appalling (although, for the matter of that, I am about as well qualified for giving an opinion on that point as a South Sea Islander); and that whenever one sees a good figure it is generally capped by a plain face; and that the pretty-faced miss almost always has her head very ill set on her shoulders, and wears a badly made gown.

"I have often wished I were a man," I say, as we turn back into the drawing-rooms, "but I never wished it as heartily as I do to-night. Even that silly-looking boy, propping himself up against the door yonder, is free to choose his partners, while I have to wait until some one or other condescendingly *fetches me out*."

"But you can always say 'No!'"

"Not in the face of this half-filled pro-gramme," I say, glancing down at it where it sprawls widely open across the front of my dress. "It looks very like an advertisement, does it not?"

"Shall I tell you something," says Paul, looking down upon me with half-pleased, half-vexed eyes. "It is great nonsense; but then you like nonsense, do you not?"

" Yes."

" Well, then, I heard one man say to another, a moment ago—' Does any one know who is that pretty little creature in the poppies ? ' And the other answered, ' No ; but I'm determined to be introduced to her before I am half an hour older.' "

" You are making it up ! " I say quickly. " Did you think it would please me ? "

" Nell," says Milly's voice beside me, " I have brought some gentlemen to introduce to you," and she goes through half a dozen introductions and sails away. My card is produced and duly written upon by them all, then they make their bows and retire.

" I should not know one of them again if it were to save my life, so it is to be hoped they will claim me all right," I say with some dismay as they vanish.

" I don't think they will forget," says Paul reassuringly. " And now here comes St. John to fetch you ; it was the third round you promised him, was it not ? "

" Our dance, I think, Miss Adair," says the little man, and I put my hand under his arm and go away, with a rueful look at Paul.

John Peel is ringing forth in glorious fashion as we enter the ball-room. Can anything be more maddening, I wonder, than good music and a bad partner? Lord St. John does not wait for an opening, but gripping me round the waist, plunges wildly into the *mêlée*. On watching him I had been struck by the way in which he appeared to *run away* from his partner: on careering with him, I find that—proud and happy as I should be to be left out of his gyrations altogether—there is no such luck, for he holds on to me like grim death, "without any regard to my squalls or my kicks" (as a poet once wrote of a victim very little worse off than I), and that fast as he tears round me I am forced into a very similar and indecently hasty appearance of likewise tearing round *him*. In vain I ask him to stop. . . . I am, indeed, too deeply engaged in the all-absorbing business of holding on, and praying that Providence will bring me out of this *galère* without the loss of my front teeth, to say much ; so on we rush, running full tilt at the company ; dashing into the couples before us, recoiling violently on to those behind; landing with convulsive energy on the wallflowers' toes, taking headers into the wall or space, pelted with blows, harassed with return kicks, abraded with sharp elbows, verily we run a race as perilous as was that of Dick Turpin, but are not, like him, clothed with honour, but disgrace!

"Stop!" I cry loudly, when we have upset our fourth couple and only saved ourselves from rolling upon their prostrate forms by a succession of aërial bounds that would not have done discredit to Taglioni. "Stop!" And being tired by his exertions, he looses me, and I tumble into a chair, and go very near to weeping. There is a smile on the countenances of the lookers on, the very wallflowers are grinning—nasty little wretches, who would not object to be twirled round like mops, rather than not dance at all! Examining into the extent of my injuries, I find that I have a lump on my forehead that will probably be black and blue to-morrow, a partially-skinned arm and a tolerably severe cut over my left elbow, which I have indeed been using as an active weapon of offence and defence, as is the wont of women-kind in a ball-room skirmish.

"Poor little soul!" says Paul's voice beside him, and looking up with eyes that are filled partly with anger, partly with tears, I see that his face is dark with wrath and that his glance at Lord St. John is of no very friendly character.

"You should have taken better care of Miss Adair," he says sternly. "Do you see how you have hurt her?"

Poor little Lord St. John! He has no idea but that he has distinguished himself in a very spirited and successful manner, and is mopping his forehead preparatory to doing it all over again.

"Is she tired?" he asks, with genuine astonishment. "And we got on so well, too!"

"She is too tired to dance the rest of this galop," says Paul impatiently. "Miss Lister is not dancing, I see. Why do you not ask her?"

Lord St. John is essentially docile, he always does as he is bid, so he fetches the young lady and starts off again with much zeal if little discretion.

"I should like to thrash that little fool," says Paul, looking at my scratched arm and making a sudden movement towards it that he as quickly checks. "Dairymaids and cooks should be his partners, not delicate little things like you."

"I have one mercy to be thankful for," I say, sitting up and putting my hand to my head to see if my poppies still bloom there: "he did not let me down!"

"Miss Lister will not be so fortunate then; for if they don't go down before they are five minutes older I am much mistaken. Look at them now!"

I do look. Lord St. John and his unhappy partner are taking a header straight down through the room; and another couple, equally daring and unconscious, are also taking a header from the opposite end; and, alas! before either couple has time to get out of the way of the other, they meet with a violent impetus that scatters all four to the winds of heaven, or rather to the polished oak shades of the earth below.

They may be severely damaged—no doubt they are; but the laugh of the multitude is ever against those who cry out under misfortune, so they all jump up again in a trice—all, that is to say, but Miss Lister, who sits on the ground and weeps bitterly, displaying a good quarter of a yard of flat ankle that considerably mars the effect of her pearly tears. In vain her unfortunate partner assures her of his sorrow in reducing her to such a plight—in vain her friends hold out friendly hands to help her up: there she sits and weeps.

"Perhaps if Oliver were to come to the rescue she would be persuaded," says Paul; and as he speaks that gallant warrior, attracted by the crowd, and not having seen the catastrophe, approaches with much interest, and peeps over. At the sight that meets his gaze—to his shame be it spoken—he turns tail and runs. "It must have been her ankle," says Paul in deep disgust. "I wonder they do not call in two stout footmen." She gets up at last, though, with unavailing tears running down her hot angry face, and her apple-blossom wreath cocked rakishly over one eye as though it rather enjoyed her miserable condition than otherwise. "Let me see your card," says Paul, stooping over it; "ours is the second from this. I see your next is with Sir William Aldous."

"Was not he the man who was all nose and no legs?" I say, considering; "or the one with a big forehead and no chin?"

"You are very disrespectful to your admirers," says Paul laughing, "considering your charms brought the assemblage together."

"My charms?" I say, laughing aloud. "Are they then *un fait accompli?* Are they placed beyond the region of doubt? Well, I am proud, really proud of the collection my charms brought together! Take me back to Milly, please, before my partner comes to fetch me."

On our way Silvia passes us on Viscount Linley's arm. His sallow face is alight with admiration.

"He seems to admire her very much," I say.

"He loves every pretty woman he sees,"

says Paul, with a queer smile, "whether she be white, brown, or black. If the love of woman is really a 'liberal education', then he reflects great discredit on your sex, child; for the older he gets the worse he grows!"

I am scarcely by Milly's side when Sir William Aldous comes to claim me for the Lancers, and I find myself excellently well-amused, for he turns out to be a fool of the finest quality and most exquisite water. All through these sober decorous old Lancers (How much longer will they be permitted, I wonder, in this age of break-downs and fast dances? The nine-teenth century stands them; but will the twentieth?) he amuses me charmingly; for fools may be divided into two classes—those who know it, and those who do not. My partner is of the latter class; therefore, since his silly remarks are always uttered with a perfect air of good faith, and are neither recalled nor repented, of, he is boundlessly fresh, inexhaustibly amusing, as no wise man could be with solid reason, admirable logic, and weighty pro and con. It is tolerably easy to guess at what a

sensible man will do, under any given circumstances; but I defy any one to fore-
cast the words and acts of a downright
talking fool. He will unconsciously say
things that are almost like flashes of
genius, his words will be the very inspira-
tion of folly, and he will scale heights and
plumb depths before which wise men have
stood silent and abashed.

The dance over, we go into the hall, and
so to the refreshment-room, where he leaves
me in a comfortable chair, and departs in
search of claret-cup. Close to me a group
of men are discussing the charms of their
late partners, with a freedom that should
delight those ladies, if they were by to
hear.

"Give you my word of honour, Dal-
rymple," says one, "she had an entirely
new set for this evening. Only had a very
few teeth left—remaining stumps were taken
out yesterday—new set put in this morning
—here to-night!"

"Don't believe any mortal woman could
stand it," says another.

"Then she's immortal, my dear fellow,"

says the first speaker, "for I know it to be a fact. She's engaged too. Rather awkward person to kiss—eh? Things may come to a dead lock."

"Or lock-jaw."

"I hope this is right," says Sir William, appearing before me. "I did not quite like the flavouring, so I have been showing the butler how to improve it."

So that accounts for the disgusted expression on Birkhead's face. Evidently he does not appreciate a fool as keenly as I do!

CHAPTER X.

"How sweet the moonlight sleeps upon this bank !
Look how the floor of heaven
Is thick inlaid with patines of bright gold."

SUPPER is over, and I have danced a great
many dances with partners, good, bad, and
indifferent, have been startled, amused,
pleased at the pretty speeches made to me,
and which I have tried hard to convince
myself are not meant in the very least,
though in my secret soul I do believe that
a few of them were not spoken in jest but
earnest; and now we have stepped out of
the crowded, noisy rooms, Paul and I, on to
the terrace, where couples are walking up
and down in the clear white light of the
moon making love, or the semblance of it,
Corydon to Phillis, and sometimes—alas, for
the order of things !—Phillis to Corydon.

Paul has stolen a warm white shawl from the back of a chair, where it had been left by an unsuspecting dowager; there will be a fine hue and cry after it by-and-by.

The night is very lovely, more like an August one than September, the air is so warm, and the perfume of the flowering myrtle wanders abroad so sweetly. Down yonder, by the trout stream, the great masses of foliage lie dark and stirless; there is not a puff of wind to rock the pigeon-cotes hung aloft in the boughs; there is no sound of insect, bird, or beast, to ruffle the silence, only the far-off swish of the sea as it softly laps the shore. Turning the corner of the house, we come to a stone parapet, that overlooks the flower garden dappled all over with flowers and melting imperceptibly into the woods, that in turn seem to merge themselves into the sea. From the bed of mignonette below comes up to us a pure, fresh breath, that recommends itself more favourably to me than any of the voluptuous heavy perfumes of the hot-house flowers we left in the room behind us.

" I wonder if Juliet had a bed of mignonette?" I say, looking out at the silver streak of sea beyond the dusky woods.

"I dare say. What made you think of her?"

"This parapet and the flower garden stretched out below. I can almost fancy I hear Romeo calling—

> 'Call me but love, and I'll be new baptized ;
> Henceforth I never will be Romeo ;'

and Juliet calling back—

> 'My bounty is as boundless as the sea,
> My love as deep ; the more I give to thee,
> The more I have, for both are infinite.'"

"Do you think any girl could love like that now-a-days, Nell?"

"Was she not very quick?" I ask doubtfully ; "do you not think it was strange she should have fallen in love with him all at once like that?"

"It is a poor love that is afraid to discover itself as soon as felt," he says, "and that beats about the bush until it is certain of the same being returned. I believe that the strongest and most enduring love is that which is sudden, or fallen into."

"I am glad they both died," I say ; "perhaps if Romeo had lived he would have loved some one else and spoilt the whole story."

"Yes, I think he would have forgotten in time and loved again, as you say; why should he not? Do you believe that a man cannot care as much the second time as the first?"

"I do not know about men," I answered; "I only know that a woman could not. Juliet would have had no second lover, I am very sure."

"If you had been Juliet," he says, stooping his head to look into my face, "and Romeo had died, what would you have done?"

"I should not have killed myself, but I should have loved him dead as passionately as I had loved him living; and no word of love from another should ever have shamed his memory."

"I am going to ask you a question, child; an impertinent one you will no doubt consider it, but I will have an answer. *Have you ever had a lover?*"

My heart stands still as I lift my

eyes to him, standing there by my side. For a moment I hesitate; then, for speaking the truth has always come more naturally to me than to tell lies, I answer, " Yes."

He turns away. " They are all alike," he mutters half-aloud, " all alike ! "

" And he makes love to you, I suppose ? "

" Yes, indeed ! " I say, with a rueful sigh, given to the memory of how bootless that love-making has proved.

" And do you like him ? "

There is a confident, half-teazing ring in his voice as he asks the question, and I turn my head away ruffled and hurt. Shall I talk over George's true, honest love ?

" Nell ! " he says, coming round to the other side and looking into my averted face, " did you hear me ? "

" Yes."

" Confess now that you do not care a straw for this— *this Lubin?* "

" Do I not ! " I answer, roused by his tone and the slighting allusion to my absent lover, who is so leal to me, and to whom I—— " There you are quite mistaken; I like him very much indeed; next to my own people I don't know any one whom——"

"Next to your own people!" he says, with a queer smile. "Would you not put the man you loved before?"

"That would entirely depend on who he was! If he were a selfish person——"

"If? Have you not made up your mind, then?"

But I do not answer him. I slip from his side and run fleetly away, and reach the ball-room before he can overtake me: certainly it was a narrow escape that time. My partner for the dance meets me as I enter, and I walk through the Lancers absently enough; fortunately, however, he has the gift of the gab in high perfection, and I am only required to throw in an occasional yes and no. We have for our *vis-à-vis* a very stout lady and a very active little gentleman, and looking upon them, I am irresistibly reminded of an elephant labouring after a flea, she is so slow he so spry; I am sure he takes a dozen steps to her one. On my left is a broad-faced young man, who wears a perpetual and uneasy smile, that neither seems able to expand into a grin or depart in peace; I have a great mind to make a face at him as we advance in the figure, and see whether it deepens or vanishes.

It is growing very late, or early; daylight will soon be looking in upon us, but the fun of the ball is at its height. Supper has made shy men bold, bold men impudent, silent men garrulous, and cheerful men harlequins; prim young women relax into hearty laughter, fast young women wax faster; admiration degenerates into flirtation, and flirtation into downright love-making; love-making, that is to say, which is born of champagne, propinquity, and opportunity— a poor imitation of the genuine article. The dowagers beam unctuously over their double chins; there is not a wallflower left to grace the wall. Have they indeed risen and *touted* for partners? Several proposals are flying about, and the general appearance of everything points to the fact that time is scurrying with flying feet, and that they who would enjoy themselves must do so speedily, or not at all.

How the society masks drop off the faces! How the true ring of the voice comes out, and the real expression of lips and eyes reveals itself! If a physiognomist could stand in our midst, how easily he would read the relaxed countenances of those present! Of some it is true there is no evil or mischief to learn, but of others much. Many of the men and women here to-night bring into society faces as carefully prepared to meet the world's eye as the clothes they wear; it is not often one can get a peep at them as they really are.

We go into the supper-room, where are congregated a good many people, drinking, talking, laughing, fanning themselves, making love, and talking scandal. Scraps of conversation come fitfully to my ears. " What colour eyes do you like best?" " Blue, like yours." " My dear Mrs. Backbite, I *saw* the man deliberately kiss her hand, and she actually looked as though she liked it!" " Yes, first-rate action. Is it true she is scratched for the Vasher stakes?" " Yes; and entered for the Vestris." " It was Vasher who sheered off, not the Fleming." "St. John says that Vasher is mad about that Miss——" (I do not catch the name). "Any one can see that." I do not hear the rest, for Paul himself stands before me.

"This is our waltz," he says. "Are you too tired to dance it?"

"No."

I put my hand in his arm, and go back to the ball-room. Already it is growing empty; some one or other has made a move, and like a flock of sheep every one is following. Willing mothers are running about after their unwilling daughters, who have, indeed, the advantage over their anxious parents, inasmuch as they can dance away from the same, "up the sides and down the middle."

Faster and faster goes the music, quicker and quicker go the flying feet; all are enjoying it with a zest that nothing, save the knowledge that it will be quickly over, could possibly give. Into the feet of some of the middle-aged waiting folk the music gets, and partners being forthcoming they essay a turn or two, at first with some shyness, much as Mr. Aminadab Sleek and Lady Creamly did in "Home," then with vigour; finally they revolve with much enjoyment, perfect in the steps of thirty years ago.

Oh, this last dance! The light, the music, the perfume of the flowers, the long harmonious movement, they are woven into one exquisite sensation that blooms for a little space and dies. And now all too soon the waltz ceases, and delivers over the girls to the custody of their mothers, and they go away torn, spoiled, draggled, with all the carefully built up finery of a few hours ago in ruins. It is always wretched work seeing the last of everything—the lights put out, the daylight on weary faces, and the winding up. So at the foot of the stairs I say good-night to Paul. But he does not take my hand, and as I turn away he walks along by my side.

"Good-night, again," I say, wearily, as I reach my door. "Oh, I am so sleepy!"

"Good-night," he says; then pressing both my hands against his lips, "Good-night, little Nell!"

CHAPTER XI.

"When Phœbus doth behold
His silver visage in the watery glass,
Decking with liquid light the bladed grass."

NINE o'clock is striking as I open my eyes, brightly, broadly awake, and rested. Sleep is a cunning fellow; he knows when his subjects have had enough of him, and when he strikes them with his fairy wand, crying, "Awake!" they only are wise who leap up and begin their day; it is the foolish ones, who do not know what is good for them, that turn away from the light, heavily courting the slumber that is not necessary, therefore will not refresh them.

Looking out of the window I discover that the morning is perfect; never did nature wear a fairer robe than she has put on to-day; and I long to be out, assisting at her morning show, brushing the dew from her meadows with hurrying feet, smelling at her freshly opened buds and flowers, taking a long draught of her beautiful, vigorous, healthy life. I have some difficulty in getting my breakfast, to which is added one welcome and one unwelcome addition in the shape of a letter from Jack and another from George. I read Jack's, the other will keep. The dear boy is coming home for a few days the end of October; he is very busy, he says, and will be very glad to see me again.

Downstairs I meet nobody, save sleepy servants, who look, poor wretches! as though they had not been to bed at all. As I open the glass door of the drawing-room, a cold, sweet breath of the sea comes faintly up to meet me, and seems to die pleasantly on this warmer air that creeps about the sunny terrace and south side of the house. The trees are still bravely clad, although the finger of decay has touched their greenness here and there into flaming scarlet and vivid yellow; the birds are singing loudly and jubilantly enough, but somehow their notes do not seem to be as sweet and joyous as they were a little while ago. To them the summer meant warmth and comfort, the fruits of the earth fed them, the nights gave them shelter, but with the first breath of the frost-king they see hunger and cold stretching out before them, and the iron hardships of the long winter, at least, so their song seems to say to me as I listen. On the upper terraces, and in the glades that the sun's eye cannot reach, since the screen of leaves above is so thickly woven, the hour might be six o'clock in the morning, not ten, and there is yet some of—

"That same dew that sometimes on the buds
Was wont to swell with round and orient pearl."

And of the few scanty autumn flowers left I make myself a posy and fasten in my belt.

I wonder why one feels so much brisker, fresher, brighter, in time of autumn than in time of spring, which is so infinitely lovelier and more grateful to us? Somehow these trees, whose leaves are dying in such splendid livery of gold and sepia, crimson

and brown, strike no pang to our hearts;
they do not suggest unpleasant thoughts
of our own decay; on the contrary, we walk
erect, and cheat ourselves with the vain
belief that, though all things fade, yet do
not we; or, at least, not now. How we
cling to our little atom of life, that is so
small and yet so huge, and, placed directly
before our eyes as it is, assumes grand
proportions that block out the far off and
dimly seen plains of eternity—very misty,
very vague, they look to our earthly, filmy
eyes. Religion bids us hold ourselves ready
to quit at any moment the world and everything we value and love; and human hearts,
recoiling, are called craven and sinful, as
though a child would go willingly from the
warm arms of the mother it trusts and is
used to, into the unknown embrace of a
veiled and shadowy stranger, that may be
more tender, more loving, more satisfying,
than the earthly mother; but, oh! the
child cannot see its face, cannot hear its
voice; it is all strange, and it turns back
trembling to the face it *knows*, just as we
who are grown up cling to life, with its

sweetness and its sorrows, its love and its suffering, and hug it to our breasts, our very own and a most familiar friend. When my time for dying comes, and I know that surely—certainly it must come some day— that I shall lie straight and still, with blank eyes and heavy-shut lids, with ears into which no common call or every-day word can enter, I hope that all my dear ones, the few that I lay in my heart, will have gone before me; then, indeed, I shall not fear to die, for where they are there will be my home.

I have fallen on sad thoughts this bright morning. Am I not, indeed, becoming somewhat sentimental? a state of mind for which I have a most hearty contempt. I will go to the kitchen garden and search for figs and pears. I have eaten three treacly-sweet figs, and am investigating the Marie Louise pears, when a voice behind me says, "Good morning!" I turn round, and there stands Paul Vasher. Is he shod with the shoes of silence, or does he wear goloshes? for I never heard him coming.

"Good morning!" I say, holding out my

hand. "I thought you were still in bed or out shooting!"

"Luttrell is lazy this morning," he says, "and nobody would turn out. Have you breakfasted?"

"An hour ago," I answer, looking at my watch; "it seemed a crime to stay in on such a morning as this, so I got out as quickly as I could."

"I hope you slept well?"

"I always do, always, that is to say, when I have nothing on my mind."

"Well, I did not sleep at all."

"Why did you not?"

"I began to think, and then it was all over."

"About bills?"

"No," he says smiling; "what made you think of bills, of all things?"

"Because they keep——" I am about to add, "mother awake," when I stop short. "Is it not very odd," I continue, as we walk along between the cabbages, "how the merest trifles that we hardly notice by day assume *gigantic* proportions at night? Do you know that all the silly things I have said and done, and all the times I have made a fool of myself, rise up before me if I am awake, and seem to pelt me? and when daylight comes they appear quite small again, and I recover my self-respect; do you ever feel like that?"

"Often enough," he says, rather sadly. "Only the blows my sins deal me are somewhat heavier than those your little white misfortunes give you. I often think though, that there is no exaggeration about those night thoughts; that things do but assume their real significance then; truer counsel comes to us in those silent hours than in the broad garish day, with its thousand sights and sounds, and words to come as a screen between us and our souls."

"Let us take comfort in that our consciences are active and healthy!" I say laughing; "it is when people do not feel their shortcomings at all that they may be considered to be in a bad way, is it not? I suppose all eminently wicked folk have no conscience at all?"

"Child," he says, looking down at me, "what a merry, heart-whole laugh you have, "any one could tell you had never lost yourself."

"Lost myself?" I repeat; "what is that?"

"Never been in love," he says slowly, and with an odd hesitation in his voice, odd by reason of his being usually so self-contained, proud, and cold.

I turn away my head that he may not see how the colour goes out of my cheeks. I am glad he thinks me so safe and untouched. No woman should wear her heart upon her sleeve for every eye to look into. . . .

"Do people give up laughing when they fall in love?" I ask. "I should have thought it would be the very reason why they should be all the happier! My sisters never wore long faces when they were engaged. I do not think I ever saw any other lovers, unless indeed one can call Silvia and Sir George lovers."

"And are they not?"

"I don't know."

My thoughts go back to that moonlight night at Charteris four years ago, when a man and woman stood face to face and

wished each other a bitter, long farewell—
ay, *they* were lovers; and a hot sharp pain
runs through my heart that I know well
enough is jealousy.

"Mr. Vasher," I say, stopping short, while
the blood leaps into my face and mounts to
my very brow, "I have something to tell
you—something I ought to have told you
long ago." He does not answer, but I see
him draw in his breath and set his lips hard,
and in his eyes there is a look of strong,
eager expectation. "That night, at Charteris, when you had that interview with
Silvia, I was hidden close to you, and saw
and heard everything."

"Is that all?" he cries, with a quick
gesture of relief, and yet a certain shame in
his face. "I thought you were going to
tell me—— So you heard our farewells,
child; were you sorry, or did you laugh?"

"It was nothing to laugh at," I say
seriously; "but I have always wanted to
tell you. I felt such a sneak, but it was
not my fault, and I thought I should vex
you so by walking out in the middle. I
wish I had never been there."

"Do you?" he says. "Why?"

"Until then I had believed in love, and that it lasted. Now I know better; and that however hotly a man may worship a woman to-day, he forgets her to-morrow."

"Not if she is worthy," he says. "Would you have him pour all his treasures into the sea? A man must be true to himself first, his love afterwards."

"And I cannot understand this distinction," I say, looking down at my flowers. "If I ever loved any one, and afterwards he proved unworthy, I should not let that turn me back. I should go on loving just the same."

"Because you have a sweet and unselfish nature, while I am selfish through and through," he says slowly. "It is a cowardly thing, is it not, to be so careful to assure one's self against loss? But I have always felt that on the woman I married depended the making or marring of my life, and— still in my own interests of course—watched natures as narrowly and carefully as a man would look to the joints of his armour before going into a battle, on the issue of which his life depended. Do you blame me that I will not sacrifice my life—I have only one, remember!—simply to gratify a woman's caprice? Can you show me a greater misery than to be bound to a person one can neither trust nor respect? With me worth ranks before beauty."

"I cannot argue," I say slowly; "I can only feel; and it seems to me that lovers once, who love each other, should be lovers always; nothing but death ought to come between."

"Then Silvia and I should be lovers now?"

"If you had loved her really, I think you would be loving her still, faults and all."

"Faults?" he repeats. "You don't understand. What if I give you the key to the puzzle? What if I tell you why Silvia's beauty moves me no jot? Why it is as impossible to me to have any love for her as to breathe life into dry-as-dust bones? Shall I tell you a story? You may suppose it to be my own, or that of any one else, just as you please."

We have come to a gnarled old garden seat, that is set where the eye can view the garden and woods and a glimpse of the sea below, and we sit down.

" Once," he says, leaning towards me and watching my face, " a man wandered over the world, searching in cultured gardens and wayside roads, at the gates of palaces and the doors of the poor, for a certain spotless, delicate flower. He saw many very like the particular blossom he was seeking, but there was always some trifling flaw, or speck, or stain, and he passed them all by, for he said to himself, ' I know that this flower exists, for other men have found it, and why should not I ? ' And at last to him also came the happy hour, and he found it. Long and carefully he watched it, lest after all it should be no more perfect and faultless than the rest ; but at last he put out his hand and, with a great rejoicing in his heart, plucked it. It was but freshly in his hand, he had scarcely tasted of its sweetness, hardly felt his soul filled with its exceeding beauty, its petals had not withered with neglect or been scorched by the hot breath of passion, when a chance blow struck it ; and, lo ! the dazzling whiteness fell from it like a veil, and there it lay, robbed of its deceitful mantle, lovely still, but speckled, tainted, soiled. No one but God knows what that man felt then. He had sought for it so long, exulted in it so deeply; he could have laid his life on its perfect purity and soillessness, and now, broken and shamed as it was, he loved it still, though he knew that he could never lay it in his breast, never wear it through life as his glory and pride; and therefore, though it nearly cleft his heart in twain to leave it, he cast it from him, and went his way alone.

"Not long afterwards, when he was in the very midst of his hard, fierce struggle to forget, he came by chance upon it, and though he knew its worthlessness, he longed after its beauty with a deep and passionate longing that nearly overcame him; and, after all, the speckled stains were faint and invisible to all eyes save his own, but his standard of purity was a high one, else had he not so long sought the one who should come up to it; and a second time he conquered this madness and went his way. Years after, when he was no longer seeking either good or evil, when his old search after anything perfect seemed faint and far away, he chanced upon a little flower that grew up sweet, and sturdy, and honest, in its quiet corner, past which the world never ran. It was not so gorgeous and stately as the tall white flower, but it had a fair, winsome face, and its clean, fresh sweetness came more gratefully to the weary, jaded man, than had ever the voluptuous beauty of the other. And though his love of the first had long faded away, this fresher, healthier love took and cast out the last fragments of a lingering, haunting memory; and his heart was as empty of all feeling for it, as though he had never loved and regretted so bitterly. And so—he was mad, you will say, for had not his experience been disastrous enough?—he longed for this little flower with a keen intensity that he had never known for the other." He pauses, and down-dropping into the silence come the exquisite notes of a bird, who seems to be singing miles above us, oh, so sweetly! in at God's gate.

"Was he quite sure this time?" I ask,

watching a little snowy sail that is scudding across the bit of jasper that shines through the trees. "Was he not afraid that this was a deception like the other."

"He was not afraid of that; he knew its nature through and through, but sometimes he feared he was too late; that another man had set his mark on that flower, and that its treasures were not for him; at others, he felt sure it was his own, and, at last, he made up his mind that he would speak and find out the truth, *and know*."

A rabbit scampering suddenly out of the bushes behind us startles me so violently that I leap up, and out of my shallow pocket fall two letters, and lie at my feet. Paul stoops, picks them up, turns to give them to me, when something in my face seems to arrest his attention, and he looks from me to George's big, bold handwriting, and from the letter back to me.

"Are either of these from your lover?" he asks, striking them with his forefinger.

"Yes."

"And he writes to you; you write to him?"

"Yes." (I have written George three bald epistles since I came to Luttrell.)

He does not speak again immediately, but his glance fell upon me heavy as a blow. Ah, me! men are hard taskmasters. Do they love us women at all, save for their own pleasure? Are they not mercilessly cruel when we make them suffer passing pain or discomfort? I want to tell him that it is all a mistake; that if George is my lover, I am not his; but somehow the words refuse to utter themselves. . . .

"I have not told you the end of my story," says Paul Vasher; "will you care to hear it?"

"If you please."

"I don't know how it was I came to tell it you, unless indeed it were to convince you that I do not love Miss Fleming. The ending is simple enough; some tales do end happily, you know."

"And it did end happily?" I ask, very low, while the dread that has for the past minutes been creeping about my heart, trembles and dies.

"Yes; I will show her to you some day."

Has the bird gone in at heaven's gate, or are my ears too deaf to hear him? What is this greyness that is creeping over land and sea? The little white sail has vanished, and the diamonds that bordered the ocean's breast have died dully out.

"I hope, sir," says a gentle voice, that sounds something like mine, "that you found her all you could wish."

Looking idly down at my lap, I see all my pretty flowers lying headless; did my fingers strip them from their stalks?

"It is cold," I say, shivering; "let us go in."

Side by side, down the green glade, we move in silence. "Oh, fool!" the trees seem to whisper as I pass. "Oh, fool!" cry the birds, in their mocking shrill voices. "Oh, fool!" cries louder and deeper my heavy, heavy heart. If I could only laugh aloud, jest, speak carelessly. . . . About fifty paces from our seat we meet Alice, fresh and fair and blooming as the morning itself. Alice is one of those few people who can look as well by daylight as wax-light. After the usual salutation—

"How pale you are," she says to me. "Why did you get up so early?"

"You forget how I danced last night," I say, turning aside to pick up my small nephew, who is rendered the freak of fortune as much by reason of the length of his swallow-tailed pelisse as by the unsteadiness of his legs. How she ever got him so far up is a mystery; how to get him down again, I find by experience, is a work of time and difficulty.

Alice and Paul are talking about the ball; she with much spirit, he with a listlessness that makes me look at him once with shrinking, perplexed eyes. For a man who is successful in his second courtship, he does not look happy; there is a dull, disappointed expression upon his face.

"It seems to me," says Alice, "that you are two very lively people; have you been quarrelling?"

A timely upset of her son takes up my attention at this moment; but I hear Paul's answer plainly enough.

"Quarrelling, Mrs. Lovelace? I think

not. I have been telling Miss Adair a story; that is all."

To Alice's sisterly looks and asides of inquiry, I turn blind eyes and a blank countenance, and presently, having guided the cherub's steps past the gold and silver fish, whose watery abode he evinces a rooted determination to share, I get away, and upstairs to my own room, and lock the door. As I kneel down by my bedside, and press my knees hard against the floor, I do not say to myself that an exquisite hope that has sprung up, at unawares, in my heart is dead; slain by a sharp, swift death that, maybe, is more merciful than a halting, lingering one. . . .

I am not conscious of thought, I only know that I thought myself rich, and that now my kingdom has passed away into other hands: my poor kingdom that was never anything but a fanciful one, and which I have seemed to see growing stately and beautiful day by day. . . . There are some miseries over which one may weep aloud with not only deep self-pity, but the pity of the world beside; there are others

over which it is a shame to make one sigh,
to drop one heavy tear, that can know of
no relief, but must be carried about with
us, like a burning cross that lies on the
naked, bleeding heart.

"Luncheon is served," says Annette,
entering half-an-hour later.

I have smoothed my untidy locks, put
on fresh ribbons, rubbed my cheeks hard
with a towel, and now I look no worse than
any other country miss, who is not used
to racketing, and who stood up for her
first real ball, and danced twenty-one
dances over-night.

"And now," I say to myself as I go down
the broad stairs—

> 'Away! and mock the time with fairest show,
> False face must hide what the false heart doth know.'

I dare say George would say my heart
was false."

CHAPTER XII.

" Where fair is not, praise cannot mend the brow."

Out in the garden I am pacing up and down, up and down through the silver bars and the dark shadows, backwards and forwards as for a wager, trying to trample out the aching pain in my heart, as many a man and woman has tried before me, and will try after me in vain. And only a week ago at this hour I was so happy, so happy! And by this day twelve months, I shall perhaps have got rid of this ugly ache, and be moderately happy again, but, oh! I never knew the prospect of a cheerful to-morrow bring any comfort to a chilly to-day; it is the present hour that we hold fast between our hands that is our care. It is a pleasant thing, is it not, to find that your heart has slipped away out of your safe keeping,

and knocked at the wrong door, and that
your affections have set in a broad,
liberal stream towards a man who wants
none of them, who has been at the pains to
tell you he is in love with somebody else?
My cheeks burn, my foot presses deep into
the grass, as I wither under the shameful
thought; taking all due blame to myself,
has he not been somewhat in fault, did he
not mislead me by his looks and words?
Bah! it was all my own wretched vanity;
could not a man be kind and friendly with
me, but I must suppose he had lost his
head, and fall in love with him myself, a
little fool! as though I had never had a
lover, or heard a love word in my life, and
was ready to leap at the ghostliest shadow
of a man's light fancy!

I stand still to think, suddenly, of how
thoroughly George is avenged, of how
I have come to suffer all the pains that
I laid on him; I can feel for him now,
my poor fellow! as I never felt before;
truly pity is sometimes a selfish thing. I
think that, considering our youth and the
few opportunities that we have had of gam-

bling, George and I show as clean a sheet of
bankruptcy in our heart affairs as could be
seen anywhere. We shall be able to mingle
our sighs and groans in a pleasing duet by
the river-side, for I know now very certainly
that, difficult as I have always found it to
look upon George as my future husband,
when nothing more than a girl's idle fancy
stood between, we are now as utterly sepa-
rated as though either or both of us lay in
our coffins.

His instinct warned him truly, when
he stood before me, and entreated me not
to come on this visit! had I not in truth
done better to stay at Silverbridge? Might
I not have come to love my yellow-haired
laddie, and never had my heart wakened by
the Prince Charming who came too late?
My heart is sore as I think of the words I
shall have to speak to him, sweet, pleasant-
sounding words, bright with truth; "*I have
fallen in love with somebody, George, who
is in love with somebody else.*" That is
plain enough at all events. I think I must
have loved that other ever since the old
Charteris days without knowing it. Was it

his memory, I wonder, that made my eyes so fastidious when they rested on George? Was I ever unconsciously comparing my fair-browed lover with the dark strong face that I had seen soften and pale under the lips of the woman he loved, and who loved him? Were George's sunny blue eyes but handsome, common-place bits of colour beside those splendid dark ones, that flash and burn and subjugate and sway my heart with their masterful will as none ever did or could?

We shall be a lovelorn assembly at Silverbridge: the thought of how everybody will be in love with everybody else provokes an unwilling smile from me. George is in love with me, I am in love with Paul, Paul is in love with somebody else: now if *she* would only come to Silverbridge and fall in love with George, we should be the most amusing *partie carrée* of lovers that the world ever saw, and our united sighs would form a high wind wherever we went. In time of drought we might go out in a body and water the land, and at all the funerals in the neighbourhood our looks would be far more grief-inspiring than any amount of well-fed, sober-faced mutes. I wonder if I shall always be able to see my misfortunes in a ludicrous light, no matter how painfully I smart under them?

Will Paul expect me to listen to the tale of his lady love's perfections? I am puzzled to know why he should have told me of her at all, for clearly he has told no one else here. Probably he has favoured me with his notice because he has all along had me in his eye as a nice comfortable sort of person to whom he can maunder on by the hour about his charmer's perfections. I told him when I came here that I would be gooseberry to him, has he taken me at my word, and is going to make a listening one of me? I have always been afraid that he would come under Silvia's influence again, but he has not.

Paul Vasher is neither a weak nor a forgiving man. I like these strong, deep natures: the impulsive, pleasant-mannered, facile folk may be twice as lovable, but they are like sand, and that which they receive quickly is as quickly effaced; while the favour of the proud, reserved man or woman is precious and rare, since it is vouchsafed to but few. I should like to know what Silvia would say if she knew? For all her indifference, I have caught some strange glances shot at Paul's unconscious face, and several times lately perceived her watching me with a keen intentness that tells a different story to her idle, listless ways, and *nonchalant*, careless speech.

How the men are laughing in the dining-room! What guffaws and explosions and exhausted roars peal forth! Something vulgar is on the *tapis*, I am certain, for I have long since learned that anything broad appeals irresistibly to man, whether he be prince or potman, prelate or parson, learned sage or simple squire; men's hearts warm to each other over a good joke, and Shakspeare might as well have written, "A touch of *vulgarity* makes the whole world kin," as "nature." In the drawing-room the married ladies are holding up their hands, and relating to each other stories tending to the discredit of their men and maids in waiting, who are, strange to say, addicted to much the same vices and weaknesses as their masters and mistresses (such presumption !), only, poor souls ! they are not delicate over them; and romance without an "h" to bless itself with does not appeal to the imagination as the more aristocratic failings of their betters do.

You, Sarah Ann, who have been discovered with Jeames's arm pressing your too adaptive form, are a bold-faced, abandoned hussey, and out you must pack without a character, and with a scanty wage; and you, Jeames, are a shameless varlet, who ought to be above such lowness, but as you are not, there is not much difficulty in prophesying your end. You neither of you seem to be aware that only rich people, high people, good people (so called from a polite fiction, for is not the best society the worst?) can be immoral with impunity, and embrace other men's wives and daughters when they please; to be wicked with safety you must roll in a carriage, and keep your unlawful assignations with a coachman and footman to vouch for your respectability. Sarah Ann is married and her husband has

left her, and Jeames is married and his wife
has left him, but as neither of them are rich
enough to procure a divorce, and since (as
I have said before) they are not in that state
of life where their flirtations would be pleasantly winked at, I fear the poor woman will
go down, down, down!

Birkhead was drunk the other night,
could anything be more disgusting? All his
life he has seen gentlemen with hard heads
drinking a great deal more than is good for
them; he has a weak one, but is indecent
enough to wish to be convivial "below
stairs" too, and, of course came to grief.
Now drunkenness, sitting hiccoughing at
the head of its table, and able to offer its
guests the choicest wines is one thing, and
drunkenness in low life, without a cellar to
bless itself with, is another. Faugh! send
him away, and let him not come 'twixt the
air and our nobility; that man will die in a
workhouse.

Silvia comes stepping across the grass all
in white; is she restless, I wonder, like me?
Bad as my thoughts are I would rather have
them than her company, so I move away

towards the terrace, but she calls to me—

"Helen Adair! Helen Adair!"

She has that most excellent thing in woman, a low, sweet voice.

"I wonder what she wants with me?" I say to myself, as I go slowly towards the seat she has taken. Our conversation has always been of the baldest; if, indeed, she can ever be said to converse with any woman.

"Did you call me?"

"Yes; sit down here for a few minutes, it is miserable out here alone. How long have you had a fancy for moonlight walks?" she asks, leaning her shapely head against the wooden seat; "for my part I always hated the moon, a great empty, bare splendour that chills one."

She shivers and draws her shawl closely about her—and, indeed, these September nights are growing treacherous. Looking down at her feet I see that she has adopted the sensible precaution of thick boots, as I have done.

"How those men are laughing," she

says, "at some racy story, no doubt. Paul Vasher's lungs seem to be in a satisfactory state. Have you and he been quarrelling?" she says, turning her head till her eyes rest on my face.

"I did not know it."

"Sir George and I have both remarked it. Until a week ago you were inseparable, now you are conspicuous by your absence from each other."

Some slight intangible insolence in her tone gives flavour to her words, and warns me that she means mischief; and, indeed, I might have known her better than to suppose that she would take the trouble to come out here to talk commonplaces; but since she has thrown the gauntlet down, I will not fear to take it up.

"You do me too much honour," I say quietly, "and him. We should never have taken the trouble to watch the affairs of you and Sir George Vestris so closely."

And as I meet her eyes full under the moonlight, I smile scornfully, securely. How heavy my heart is she shall not know, and of her pity I shall have none, therefore rally to my side coolness, disdain, indifference. As I look into her face with a fuller knowledge of the truth than she possesses, I can see clearly enough that she believes me to be *her rival*, that she is jealous; I see that the love Paul believed to be long dead lives as fiercely and hotly in her as ever, and at this moment we read each other's hearts, see each other as we really are . . . henceforth no shams or subterfuges will rise up between Silvia Fleming and me! She looks away.

"May I then be allowed to congratulate you on your felicity?"

With the intonation she gives these words, they sound more like a menace than a politeness.

"When you will condescend to explain yourself, I may possibly be able to answer you, Miss Fleming." (How I must have disliked this girl all my life, to flare up so heartily at a moment's notice!)

"You are rather slow of comprehension to night! I allude, of course, to your engagement with Paul Vasher."

A smile parts my lips as I listen to her.

How sweet those words sound, spoken even by an enemy's tongue! For a moment I forget the woman by my side, and that she waits my answer; I am looking at a happy, far-away picture, that makes my eyes ache with longing; only in dreamland does it exist, in reality it never will.

"And it is so," says a low, breathless voice by my side. "You sit there smiling; you dare to mock me with your gladness." . . .

Her words come hurrying out as though past her control. For the second time in her life, Silvia drops the mask before me; for the second time in my life I see her as she is.

"Let me tell you this, Helen Adair, that you will never be Paul Vasher's wife, never!"

"I have not aspired to that honour," I answer quietly; "do you? I should not, were I you!"

"You have such faith in your powers of keeping him?" she asks scoffingly.

"I have much faith in the power of the woman he loves. Pray, do not put yourself out!" I say, looking away from her pale face to the pearly sea beyond; "we need not quarrel over Paul Vasher, since he is neither yours nor mine."

"Not yours?" she repeats, staring at me, while a swift surprise dashes all the triumphant scorn out of her face, "whose is he then?"

"Some stranger's."

"And her name?"

"I do not know it."

"And so he was amusing himself with you all that time?" she says.

"You can call it that, if it so pleases you."

"And he told you this himself?" she says.

But I do not answer, and she goes on like one who is thinking hard and deep.

"I do not believe it. It is you whom he loves. . . . I have watched him——"

I turn my head away, that she may not see the pallor that has crept over my face. Others were deceived by his manner to me, then; I have not been the only mistaken one.

"It is all the same," she says, indifferently. "I told you that you should never be Paul's wife, and you never shall, but neither shall any other woman."

"Are you mad?" I ask contemptuously, for the shameless, godless selfishness of the creature angers me deeply. Does she give one thought to him? She would trample his life beneath her feet rather than see another woman take the place she once filled; that which she calls love is one corrupt, foul adoration of self.

"I am glad you love him," she says, with a malicious cruelty of look and word that sets ill upon her fair, innocent-looking beauty. (No wonder Paul thought he had found his spotless white flower at last when he beheld her; no angel could boast a more perfectly fair face!) "Glad that there is some one who will suffer as I have suffered, endure what I have endured, weary for him as I have wearied."

"Hush!" I say, rising and lifting my hand; "do not dare to link my name with yours, or call your wicked passion for Paul Vasher *love!* You, who would sacrifice his whole life to grasp your own paltry, pitiful

wish—you dare to call that loving him?
No wonder you never kept him! Thank God,
I can love him better than that! I wish
I had been lovely, for his sake. . . . I should
have liked to be good, for his sake. . . .
He might have loved me then, but even as
it is, and though he never loved me, while
he loved you once (you should never forget
that), my love for him has only taught me
sweet and tender and sorrowful things; it
has not set a flood of wild, impious passion
ravening through my heart, as it has done
through yours. If I could have my empty
heart back again I would not, for if he has
brought me pain he has also given me an
exquisite happiness. And since you never
truly loved him, or as he ought to be loved,
I tell you now that, however low you stoop,
you will never win him back, though Satan
were your bondsman and delivered Paul
Vasher's body over to you; you could not
touch his soul, his mind, or his heart, they
are dead to you now and always. And now
go your way, fight your fight, do your worst
—win him if you can, Silvia, but if the
memory of the girl he loves do not protect

him from your unwomanly pursuit, believe
me when I say, that in his integrity you
have an enemy that will never yield to you.
By fair means you will never win him; from
foul ones may God protect him."

And I move away and leave her with that
faint, wintry, strange smile on her face that
I have so often tried to read and cannot.
How cool and peaceful the sleeping garden
looks! how fair the silver-braided sky! how
hot and angry is my passionate, indignant,
outraged heart! It was hard enough to
bear my shame of lovelessness in my own
eyes; it is something harder to have that
sneering, evil woman speak openly of it.
For she is wicked, I know it now, and that
the intangible dislike and distrust I have
always had for her is a well-grounded
one, and that she means mischief to the
man she professes to love. Does she love
him, though? There was more of hate
than tenderness in her voice just now.
How can she reach or do him harm? A
woman is so bound by the trammels of
society, she cannot watch and baulk him in
life as a man might do; perhaps after all it

is mere empty talk and babble; and, granted that she has the wish to cross him, she is not likely to have the power. She seemed in earnest, but she was jealous; I saw it in her eyes, and that threw her off her guard and made her talk wildly.

We must have looked very nice just now —two women quarrelling over one man! There is an intense vulgarity in the situation, whether the actors be clad in silk and velvet, or homespun and duffle-gray; perhaps though, the fact of his being not in the least in love with either of us somewhat lessens the disgrace. And all through my night dreams, ringing now near, now far away, sometimes in my ears, sometimes seeming to call faintly across the long years, comes a bitter, silvern voice, saying, "*You will never be Paul Vasher's wife—never.*"

CHAPTER XIII.

"Sir, the year growing ancient,
Nor yet on summer's death, nor on the birth
Of trembling winter—the fairest flowers of the season
Are our carnations and streaked gillyflowers."

"What is that?" says Milly, pausing on her way upstairs.

"Can it be the ghost?" I ask, standing still to listen likewise.

Luttrell Court, like all other respectable family mansions, possesses its ghost; and an exceedingly ill-conditioned one this particular spirit is: given to heaving up beds (and their occupants) in the dead of night, dashing down cart-loads of crockery outside chamber doors, beating members of the family with invisible whips, and boxing the ears of trembling footmen in dark corners, or so those gentlemen aver.

"I don't think a ghost could give such

a substantial groan as that," I say ; and indeed, as we ascend, a succession of wails, sighs, and squeaks float out to meet us, that could not reasonably be supposed to proceed from the throat of that uncanny, fleshless, bony, counterfeit of a human being, that we call a ghost. The mysterious sounds issue from the yellow room, and Milly pushes the door open, and stands on the threshold. No poor daylight spirit is answerable for the hullabaloo ; but on a stool, before an open harmonium, sits a real tangible human being, who is rolling from side to side, in an ecstasy of delight at the hideous discord he is evoking. He wears a smart grey and scarlet livery, his silk calves are *en evidence;* he is, in short, one of the footmen, who has apparently a taste for music, and who believes Milly to be miles away at the present moment.

Some terrible instinct makes him turn his head, and standing behind him, he sees —his mistress.

"May I ask," inquires Mrs. Luttrell, "if I hired you to act as my servant, or to play on my harmonium?"

The man gazes wildly at the ceiling and the floor alternately, as though he prays Heaven to either draw him up by the hair of his head, or pull him down out of sight by his heels.

"I thought you were out, madam," he stutters, casting his eyes wildly to and fro.

"Another time," says Milly; "will you make sure? Go."

He vanishes like a stone shot from a catapult.

I look at Milly in amazement at her moderation, but suddenly recollect that the detected performer is devotedly attached to the small heir of the house, and carries him about by the hour: a royal road, that, to his mistress's favour.

"That man is a character," she says, as we go away.

"He certainly has a soul above his station," I answer, laughing, as I turn into my room to lay aside my hat. Shall I lay it aside, though? It is only five o'clock. I can do without my tea and the clack of tongues in the drawing-room; besides, the gentlemen have come in early, and I have no mind to spend an hour in trying to run away from Paul Vasher. Why does he seek me so persistently, I wonder? To make a confidante of me, I suppose; but, at any rate, I have never given him the chance; and during the last week I have become so adroit at dodging and avoiding him, that I am sure I shall find my experience useful when I go home, and have to circumvent the governor.

As I stand before the table considering, my eye catches the reflection of my face in the looking-glass, and startles me, it is so pale, so sad, so dull. I used to have such a merry, saucy face, folks said; but now, there are dark shadows under my eyes, and a close, folded look about my mouth, as though it rarely knew smiles or laughter now. Verily my story is writ upon my face, people will begin to pity me next, O heavens! and I must bear it, since there is no means of forcing the body into subjection, even if one can the spirit.

At the end of the corridor is a door by which the grounds can be reached, and I leave the house, and climb to the upper walks and terraces. I should like to go down to the sea, but it is too late to go alone; and upon its shore I could not be more lonely than I am up here. I come to the seat where Paul Vasher and I sat a week ago—only a week! And it seems a year. Everything looks different to what it did on that morning: a faint chill bleakness lies over the landscape, the trees shiver a little as the leaves fall rustling to the ground, the bit of sea in the distance is not blue at all, but a dull greyish-green; the birds are all cross, or asleep, and there is no pleasant hum of insects on the evening air. Perhaps it is I who am out of sorts, not Nature. When we begin to study the passions, can we indeed go hand in hand with her as when her gentle lore and tender secrets were all the wisdom we sought, when her peaceful voice seemed satisfying and sweet to us? We cannot hear it clearly when louder and more selfish voices are beating at our ears and echoing in our hearts. Some day I shall come back to you, oh! nurse-mother; but not now, not to-day. Give me a little while to strive with this passionate, restless heart. It will wear itself out quickly enough, never fear.

On my way, I have pulled a handful of late carnations, and some of Shakspeare's streaked gillyflowers, and I am smelling at them idly, when a fragrant whiff of another sort floats up to me—that of a cigar. This is a remote corner, and people rarely come up so high as this, so I give it no thought, and have closed my tired eyes, and am looking inward at the vista stretching out before me of endless, empty, dull to-morrows, when footsteps, brushing through the short grass, make me open them suddenly, and there stands Paul Vasher.

For a moment I stare at him without speaking, then—"I think I have been asleep!" I say, starting up; "and it must be quite tea time, time to go in!" As I turn to go he puts out his hand and lays it on my arm.

"Is this game of hide-and-seek to go on for ever?" he asks sternly (a moment ago his face was overspread with a swift gladness). "Am I always to be avoided by you in this way, morning, noon, and night?"

(I am in for it!—he is determined to make a listening gooseberry of me, willy-nilly.)

"If you call drinking tea——" I begin; then, looking up by accident and catching his eye, I stop short: evasions are always worse than useless with him.

"Your tea can wait," he says; "and you shall not go until you have answered me."

"Shall not! Who will prevent me?"

"I will."

For a moment I look straight at his resolute face, and bent brows; then I sit down again and wait for him to begin.

"I want to know," he says, standing before me, "what you mean by behaving in this way to me?"

My hands are locked fast together, my gillyflowers lie in my lap, my cheeks could grow no paler than they were before: if only my lips will keep steady, and my eyes tell no secrets——

"In what way, Mr. Vasher?"

"In never speaking to or looking at me; in never giving me a single chance of a few words alone with you—though Heaven knows I have worked hard enough to compass it. Could you have treated an enemy with more coldness and disdain? And I have been your friend, child, for many long years."

Yes, I have been wrong, as usual. I ought to have met him just the same as I did before he told me his story; instead of which, I have left him to guess the miserable truth; and now, no doubt, he pities me. . . . But I could not do the other: my strength did not go so far as that.

"You have always been my friend," I say gently. "I know it, but—you will not be angry with me?"

"Angry? No!"

"When you told me that you loved somebody, I thought you would always want to be talking about her, like other lovers, and that you would expect me to listen; and I always was a bad listener; anyone who talks as much I do, must be; and so—and so I avoided you. Besides, you can always think of her, you know; and that must be better than praising her to me, who never saw her."

"And this is the truth, the whole truth,

and nothing but the truth?" he says. Then, as I do not answer, for his searching voice arraigns me before my own conscience as having answered disingenuously: "Would it bore us so much if we were to exchange confidences—you about *him*, I about *her?*"

"Make as many as you please to me," I answer steadily, "and I will listen; but I have none to give you in return."

"None?"

"None."

"You used not to be so secret."

"Am I bound to give an account of myself to you?"

"I will have no more of this miserable uncertainty," he says suddenly. "Tell me, child, are you engaged to that man at Silverbridge?"

"That is a matter that concerns myself only."

"Are you, or are you not?" he asks again, while the veins rise in his forehead like cords, and his hand clenches.

I may as well tell him after all: why should there be any mystery over it? It can make no possible difference to him or any one else.

"No. But there is a kind of promise between us."

"A *kind* of promise? Tell me what it is?"

"When I was fourteen I gave him my word of honour that when I was eighteen year's old and six months I would marry him if——"

"If!" he repeats quickly. "Go on!"

"I did not see any one I liked better."

"Indeed! And are the six months up?"

"No."

He draws a deep breath; and then in the voice of a man who puts a strong restraint upon himself, says, "Tell me one thing now: Do you love him?"

"You ask too much," I answer, turning my pale face away. "What is it to you whether I love him or no?"

And then, against my will, I lift my eyes to his, which are deep and tender with a warm love-light . . . though he is speaking to me, he is thinking of her; and somehow the thought of her riches and my heart-bareness unnerves me, and my lips quiver, and slow, painful tears fill my eyes.

"You poor, little white blossom," he says, casting himself down on the seat beside me. "Nell, Nell! are you fretting after that Silverbridge man?"

He is looking into my face with a passion of eagerness that startles me, still thinking of her, I suppose.

"I will be good," I say, as two big tears fall with a heavy splash on my clasped hands. "Do not be afraid, I am not going to cry any more. . . . I will listen to you patiently, if you would like to have a comfortable talk about her."

"I shall keep you to your word presently," he says; "meanwhile you have not answered my question."

"I will not," I answer with spirit. (How dare he torment me in this way?)

"Will you make me a promise then?"

"Tell me what it is first."

"I cannot. Will you promise?"

There is nothing more to tell—he knows about George; is it worth while to bandy words about a trifle? And I am longing to get away.

"I promise," I say, listlessly.

"Then, when we are both at Silverbridge —for I have a fancy for hearing you tell me where I met you first, in the field of rye— you will tell me the name of the man you love."

I sit silent, pale as death. Is it kind, or manly, or fair of him to trap me thus?

"I break my promise," I say firmly, "although I never broke one before."

"It is too late, now," he says; "you are bound. You never failed in truth yet, child; are you going to begin now?"

But I do not answer.

"I think I never told you the name of my little girl? I will tell it you when you keep your promise to me—when we stand face to face in the place where I saw you first."

Ay! I see the scene clearly enough, the two figures, the shamed confession, the truth uttered as before God, the cart before the horse—the amazement of the man, who with all his faults, was never vain or coxcomb. But that hour shall never come to either him or me.

"Although I have asked you so many

questions," he says, "you have never asked me one about my sweetheart. Why do you not?"

"How tall is she?" I ask, looking up at the chilly leaves as they rustle softly down—down—down, like silk, to the ground. Since he wishes to talk I will put him through a whole catechism of questions, and, by haphazard, I begin with the one that loveless Elizabeth asked of her beautiful rival Mary.

"Just as high as my heart."

"Of what colour is her hair?"

"Brown, with a warm ruddy golden tinge running through it; it is all over little billows and cunning waves and ripples—the softest and prettiest head!"

"And her eyes?"

"She has two sweet, serious, saucy, tender grey eyes; they tell a different story every minute, but they are always true to her thoughts, which are honest; her face is the mirror of her heart, which is pure."

"Is she fair?"

"She has the whitest, softest neck and

throat and hands I ever saw. She looks as though she were made to be kissed and spoiled."

"And her mouth?"

"Not very little, but the sweetest I ever saw; and she has a dimple set at each corner."

"Is she merry?"

"You should hear her laugh! But she can be sober; sometimes I watch her face with fear, it is so sad."

And so this is why he has taken notice of me; this is why he has sought my society—because I am a plain likeness of, because I reminded him of, her. My hair, too, is rich brown; and I have green eyes, while hers are grey—not much difference there; and I used to have some dimples, I think, not so very long ago.

"And does she love you?"

"I will tell you that when you tell me what you have promised to tell."

"And you love her?" I ask, while a bitter, jealous pain creeps about my heart, and stabs it through and through while every pulse of my body seems to stand still awaiting his answer. . . .

"Do I not? God knows!"

"You are a brave man," I say, smiling with pale lips. "Are you not afraid to risk your life's happiness so utterly?"

"Is any man wise who loves? But I am not afraid: she is honest to the core, and could no more play one false than she could alter her innocent face."

"God send you happiness with her!" I say gently, and rising I go away through the silent glades, and leave him sitting there alone, with his pleasant thoughts for company, and, maybe, a pictured girl-face to murmer fond love-words over—to press close kisses on, with a chafed, angry impatience that the warm living lips are not under his own instead of the silent painted ones.

CHAPTER XIV.

"If he would despise me I would forgive him; for if he love me to madness I shall never requite him."

" GOOD-BYE!" says Paul Vasher, as he stands on the step of the railway carriage with my hand in his. "I am coming home in a day or two, and I shall then keep you to your promise."

I do not answer or look at him, although I feel his eyes searching my face. The guard waves his flag; Alice kisses her hand from the distant carriage — " Good-bye ! good-bye ! " a swift glance at Paul's dark face, a wave of the hand to Alice, and I am off, either to render up my valueless body at Silverbridge Station at 5.25, or make an unsightly corpse on the top of the engine boiler or thereabouts.

There was a horrible railway accident a

little while ago, and following that another and another. They have come hurrying after each other so fast that men going a journey wear sober faces, and enter a railway carriage with an ugly presentiment of its being a probable tomb, and are haunted with dread visions of a fast train dashing up behind, or a slow one right in the path in front, and cannot settle to their newspapers and slumbers as usual. What a pity it is bridges are not built higher and people cannot travel outside trains as they do on coaches; one would at least be able to keep a look out and see if Nemesis were overtaking us, and have a chance for our lives, instead of sitting stived up, blind as moles, helpless as infants, awaiting the crash that shoots us in one awful moment into eternity. If I come to grief to-day it will be alone, for I have a compartment all to myself, and can walk about, yawn, stretch, lounge, even laugh or cry, if it so pleases me.

Can it be only a month ago that I sped past those prim hedgerows and fields, with the ruminating cows and insensate children, who wave their dirty bits of rag at the train as it rushes by? It is thirty-one days by the almanac; but when I last came this way I was eighteen years old, and young for my age; now I feel fifty at the very least, and old for my age. By the time I really am fifty, I suppose I shall feel a hundred, and by the time I reach three score and ten—bah! It is a nasty thought that I may possibly live to that age, and live without teeth, taste, hearing, seeing, enjoying, without memory even.

As the day goes on a thought that has been lurking in some back lumber-room of my memory, forced thither by my will, steps nimbly out and stares me evilly in the face: I have to tell George. I know what I have to say to him well enough, but that does not make it any the better; and even when that terrible wrench is over, there will be the long inevitable afterwards. If only there were some city of refuge to which rejected lovers might flee, and be kept there until they had made up their minds it was no good to sigh after what they could not get! It is bad enough to say *no* over and over again to a man without having the word crystallized into a two-legged illustration who struts up and down your little stage an image of despair, and never for a moment permits you to forget that your being such a wretch to him has brought him to this miserable pass! I can feel for him now, poor George! as I little thought I ever should. Some men might be glad that I should know something of the pangs they had suffered; but George is not one of those—there never was any selfishness in him: I should have cared for him more, perhaps, if there had been. I am glad that I know the truth about Paul; that I can take my lot and look it fairly in the face, and know that if no better, still no worse can befall me. Oh! it is easier to endure the long barren bondage from which there is no escape, than to exist trembling on the frail support of a hope that may vanish and leave the horizon more utterly dark than it was before. I wonder how soon he will bring his wife home to Silver-bridge? I wonder how soon he will call upon me to fulfil my promise? He may call upon me, but I will not go: in the field of rye alone he vowed to receive it, and thither to meet him my steps shall never turn.

I walk restlessly up and down the swerving carriage—for the train is express, and we are racing against time—then sit down and pull out my letters received this morning. That from mother contains news that a month ago would have driven me wild with excitement, that a few years ago would have made Jack and me happy as king and queen, but now brings no shock of surprise, pleasure, or expectation; indeed, until the present moment, I have scarcely thought about it. The news is this: papa is going away, a long, long journey to Australia, and he will be away many months. I do not quite understand why he is going; it is something about money, and perhaps he is tired of staying quietly at home (he was a great traveller in his youth); at any rate he is going in about three weeks, mother says. What a time the young ones will have of it! To Jack and me, this gift of the gods comes too late. Now if such a chance as this had only been given to us

while we were young, we would have got
into every bit of mischief the place con-
tained, and possessed consciences clear of
ever having missed a single opportunity
of evil-doing when he returned! As it is,
with no one to harry and vituperate me,
with no one to drive me out for walks, or
compel me to overlook the morals and
manners of the boys, or labour daily at the
dry pump of conversation, I shall become
a drivelling willow-wearing lack-lustre-eyed
damsel for folks to mock at. I shall hang
out all the forlorn insignia of the love-lorn
maiden—shall I? never! If the roses will
not come back to my cheeks, the smiles
shall to my lips; I will be as merry and
noisy and saucy as ever I was, before people; I will defy any one to pry into my heart
and see what is there; and that peace will
come to me after a while I doubt not.

I wonder where Silvia is now, and
what she is doing? She left the day
after our conversation in the garden, and
we never met again. Sir George Vestris
remained one day after her departure. If
she cast him on one side, as report says

she casts all her other lovers, he took his punishment quietly and gave no sign.

Alice goes to-morrow. She has asked me to go and stay at her country house for Christmas; and perhaps, as papa will be away, I may be able to go. My sisters have pressed me hard with their questions about Paul, but I have managed to keep them off. They are puzzled, I think, as well they may be.

My journey's end comes at last, and at 5·35, reasonably punctual, according to the notions of country station-masters, the train reaches Silverbridge. There is mother in the pony-carriage; and on the platform, broader, bigger, more swaggering than ever, is the Bull of Basan; but Corydon, where is he? Invisible, thank Heaven! I jump out quite briskly. If young men whose attentions are unwelcome only knew how they endeared themselves to the objects of their affection by their absence, they would surely practice the virtue much oftener! I give mother and Basan a vigorous hug; then, my box having been duly produced and handed over to the dog-cart in waiting, we set out, mother and I, side by side, Basan occupying an abased and harassing position between the reins.

"My eye! How white you are!" he remarks at once. "Just look at her, mother!"

She looks at me with the anxious perfect love that no earthly face save a mother's ever wears, and says, "So she is. The dissipations have not agreed with you, dear. We must nurse you up now you have come home." And I know that in her gentle heart she is meditating a course of port wine and rum-and-milk.

"I say, Nell, have you heard the news?" asks Basan, dodging an insinuating irruption of leather into his right eye. "Won't we have a time of it—eh, Nell?" But mother shakes her head a little sadly.

"Poor papa!" she says; "he is very sorry to go away and leave us all." I stare at mother. Can she be *joking?* Can she mean (oh, the idea is too ridiculous!) that he *likes* us, that he is sorry to go away from us? I look at Basan. His mouth and eyes are as round as mine. We have the two longest tongues in the family, but the notion has sobered him as well as me. Papa sorry to leave us! The idea is so amazing that it literally strikes us dumb. "And how are Alice and Milly and the babies?" asks mother; and for the rest of the drive our talk is nothing but question and answer.

At the house door are drawn up the young ones, whose shouts of welcome attest without any need of inquiry, that at the present moment papa does not pervade these parts; and as I embrace them all round, I find it in my heart to wish there were even more of them, that Jack stood near for me to put my arm round his neck, that pretty Dolly was "finished" and sent home from school. They escort me to my room in a body, and make themselves very happy and busy until nurse appears to welcome me, and sweep them all away.

"Eh! but your stay has done you but little good, Miss Nell!" she says, as she stands before me. "Maybe you've been fretting after your lover, honey?"

"No, no," I answer, pressing my lips to

her brown wrinkled cheek. "I have been gay, nurse, amusing myself."

"And if that's amusing yerself, my dearie, you had better have stayed at home," she says as she goes away.

I have removed my dusty travelling-dress, and am drinking tea and eating chicken, when the trot of horses' hoofs comes up the avenue, and in another moment George and my father appear on horseback. Already! I had hoped for a little grace—just a little time to draw breath and gather up my strength. He evidently knows I am here, for he is casting his eyes over the house in the aggressively eager manner all unfavoured swains affect. It is your lover who knows he is kindly welcome, that walks in lightly and easily, sure of seeing his lady-love in good time. Although I have precipitately rolled off the window-seat, tea-cup and all, I have an uneasy feeling that he is looking at me through the bricks and mortar, and that his importunity will *compel* me into his presence whether I will or no.

When papa appears upon the scene it is

one of the rules of the family for everybody to turn out and see what he will do next. From the force of habit, therefore, I go to the top of the stairs and peep over. He is in the hall, inquiring how many hours I intend to spend in "figging" myself up. Re-assured at finding him in his normal state of temper and character—for that other phase, as suggested by mamma, is too horribly subversive of all our traditions to make me feel anything but uneasy—I return to my room to finish my toilette, and in another minute am in the dining-room, standing before the gentlemen.

My peck at papa's cheek is soon made; and then George takes my hand with a gladness in his face that I turn away my eyes from beholding. After all he only says, "How do you do?" and when I have answered "Quite well, thank you," and told him that my journey was tolerably pleasant, our exchange of words ceases, and the conversation is sustained by him and the governor. The latter going away shortly, however, on some (probable) deed of vengeance, the young man comes quickly over

to me. How frank, and fearless, and handsome he looks!—a better looking man than
Paul, the world would say.

Can you tell me, George, why you
never made me love you?—why, when my
heart was empty, you could not fill it?
Was the fault yours, or mine?

"How I have missed you!" he says,
looking into every line of my face with
greedy love. "How pale you are, Nell, and
how pretty—prettier than when you went
away, I think!"

"No, no," I say, while a pained, miserable
flush creeps slowly up to my brow; "I never
was anything to look at, George; no one
ever thought so but you."

"Did they not?" he says quickly. "I
am glad of that. I grudge every admiring
look a man casts on you, Nell. I wish you
could not be fair in any one's eyes but
mine, then they would not want to take you
away from me."

"That is kind to me," I say, smiling.
"However, you have your wish; *no one*
ever wanted to take me away from you."

"Thank God!" he says, with a deep

thanksgiving in his voice that is almost solemn. "And so you have come back to me, my own little sweetheart, never to go away from me any more!"

"Hush!" I say, turning deadly pale. "Is not that papa?"

"I don't care if it is—Nell——"

"I am going now," I say, starting back. "I cannot stay now. To-morrow afternoon at four I will be by the brook."

"To-morrow!" he says below his breath; and the rapture in his eyes makes me shiver. "I have waited so long, dear, and now——" and on his face is a look of such utter, pure content as makes his beauty something to marvel at.

Ay, to-morrow! and ere the sun has set a few words will have dashed it all out—all the sweetness of his hope's fruition—all the reward of his long, faithful service; and never, I wis, on this side of the grave, will my lover's face again wear the look it wears to-night. . . . Somehow I creep away and up to my own room, where a bitter anguish tears and rends me, heavier than all the pain I have suffered in this task set to my hand;

and until to-night I have thought almost lightly of his misery, wearily and continually of my own.   Human beings are very selfish —the pain they do not see they do not believe in or heed ; it must be placed before their eyes for them to feel the mournfulness and pity of it in their hearts.   If only I had hearkened to George's words that day when he stood under the trees and entreated me not to go away, or, if I went, to bind myself by a promise, there would be two miserable people less on God's earth to-night.

"Supper is ready!" cries Basan, bursting wildly in an hour later ; and I lift my head from the window-sill, and smooth my hair, and go down to a meal that fills me with a blank sense of amazement, it is so constrained, so unnatural.   The sociable freedom of the Luttrell table, and to which I have grown accustomed, opens my eyes to the wretched discomfort here : the few and forced words, the abuse of the servants, the perpetual looking out for imaginary faults in dishes and attendance, the unmannerly manners.   Towards the end of supper, a slight *contre-temps* occurs, for Basan being ordered in a voice of thunder to ring the bell, he starts up, poor willing youth, with extraordinary celerity, and not spying a large silver dish-cover lying near him, plants a well directed kick in the centre of its hollow body, which sends it flying across the room into the fire-place, where it lodges amid a crash of falling irons.

"Dolt! booby! fool!" yells papa, bounding in his chair; and Basan returns to the table covered with shame and confusion.

I wonder if papa will pay some family in Australia so much a week for permission to call them names? It would be hard upon him to have all his little comforts cut off at once. Supper over, poor Basan goes to bed (I wish I might), mother works, papa smokes his pipe, and I make spills, a suitable and becoming occupation for a young woman in his estimation, but one that I never excelled at, for laboriously as I roll and roll at them, they never have nice taper points or strong backs. Jack's are as stiff as pokers. How I hate these silent dreadful after-supper hours. How Alice and Milly hated them in their turn! How the young ones look forward to them with dread! In summer time it is not so bad—we are out till supper; but in autumn and winter our evil days begin, for immediately after tea we all have to take our work and sit round the table, while papa reads his newspaper; or rather, we used to, for they are all away now, the married sisters, and Jack, and Alan, and Dolly. As I look round the empty table, I seem to see us all as we sate night after night, mute as fish, but engaged in twenty reprehensible modes of passing the time.

How difficult we sometimes found it to restrain our hysterical giggles! Is there anything on earth more irrepressible or catching than a giggle! And never so irresistible as when one knows that it is as much as one's life is worth to indulge it. Once out of the room, and free to laugh as much as we pleased, we felt no inclination to do so; it was only down there, when our spirits were so tightly bottled up, and we were denied all natural vent for them, that we felt so riotous. Making faces was a favourite amusement, and in the art we all attained a fine proficiency; and quick as lightning we often had to be in regaining our personality when papa turned his head to look at us. Pinches, tweaks, and nips, were given and exchanged with a Spartan fortitude, that should prepare us in some measure for the hardships of life. But our great and mighty temptation was to throw paper pellets at the place where the hair grows thin on papa's head. How often have we sat round the table, pellets in hand, and longed to launch them, certain that we could hit that little patch with a most delicate precision. . . .

Well! I am likely to sit here making spills for a very, very long while. By the time I am an old maid I suppose I shall have made *millions*. Papa asks no questions about his daughters and their spouses; so, when I have told him that they are all well, and that Luttrell Court is a fine place, my stock of conversation is exhausted. At half-past ten I say good-night, and take my bed-room candle thankfully; but oh! there is little rest for me, for does not a bitter task await me on the morrow? and in the long days to come is there so much as a shadow of any pleasant thing that is likely to befall me?

CHAPTER XV.

"Shall I command thy love?   I may :
Shall I enforce thy love?   I could :
Shall I entreat thy love?   I will."

FOUR o'clock struck ten minutes ago ; but I am not at the rendezvous. I am loitering slowly along the meadows that lead to the running brook, and I am possessed by a keen overmastering inclination to turn round and run home again as fast as ever I can pelt. As yet, however, I have not forfeited my claim to valour, and as I go along, scarcely dragging one foot after the other, I look idly about me. This last September day is very different to that one little more than two months ago, when I wore my wreath of flowers, and later when I told George, with such grand triumph, that I was " going away." Then the world was

all quivering lights and dancing shadows.
Nature was gay and *debonnaire* with her full
summer's smile; now she seems to have
unfolded her arms to let autumn's chill
breath steal over her warm beautiful breast.
The sunlight does not brood over the earth
as it did then; rather it seems woven into a
dainty network that hovers over the distant
woods; and through the still clear air, the
far-off beeches gleam like jewels of gold and
amber. Over all there is that nameless
silence that spring and summer with their
warm bustling life never know; and the few
remaining flowers seem to be dying sorrow-
fully, while the fallen and falling leaves
cast their faint impalpable scent of decay
abroad. And now my heavy feet have
brought me within sight of the brook, and
of a man who stands by its side waiting;
and once again the irresistible inclination
to take flight, even at this eleventh hour,
possesses me; but remembering that if I
do shirk my evil task now, I cannot get out
of fulfilling it in the future, I walk quickly
on, and he, spying my approach, comes
forward to greet me.

" My darling," he says, and takes my two
bare hands and kisses them; and I look up
into his face, without a smile, without a
word. But he is very blind, he does not see,
does not heed. " You have come to tell me
that you will make a happy fellow of me at
last? "

But I draw my hands out of his, and
hide my face in them, shivering.

" Are you sorry, dear? " he asks gently.
" Are you afraid? It must seem strange
to you to promise yourself to any one—to
a stranger: you have always been so fond of
your own people; but I will be as careful
over you, Nell, as gentle———. You do not
doubt that I can make you happy? "

Then, as I do not answer or lift my face,
he goes on—" I have waited so long for
this hour, Nell, for so many weary, weary
years, sometimes I thought it would never
come. If any one wants anything as badly
as I want you, he rarely gets it; and you
know I have never had any one to care for
but you—neither mother, sister, nor brother,
and I have often noticed that when a
man centres his whole happiness in one

object it is taken from him. That is why I have always so feared, Nell, that some one would come and take you away from me. That was why I hated your going to Luttrell; for I thought all men must love you as I did, and perhaps a stranger would take your fancy. But when you told me yesterday that no one loved you but me, when I knew that my darling had come back to me safely, then, Nell, my heart was at rest, and I knew a perfect happiness, than which earth could give me no better, not if you were my own true wife, love, and bore my name. . . . I believe I thanked God." The reverent, simple voice ceases for a moment. "And now," he says, drawing my hands gently away from my eyes with one hand, while he gathers me to him with the other, "I have my reward; have I not, my darling?"

Ay! he has his reward, as I recoil from his embrace, slip away out of his arms, and stand looking at him with a measureless suffering in my eyes, with a deadly pallor on lips and cheek. A faint dread comes into his face, and dashes the surpassing brightness out; a terrible suspicion grows in his eyes, and dwells there. With that look upon him I can tell him better than I could a moment ago, when his beautiful face was all transfigured with its great happiness.

"I do not love you," I say in a whisper; "but love has come to my heart." . . . And then I cover up my face that I may not see his, and turn away.

For a moment there is a deadly waiting silence; then—

"Some one has stolen her from me!" he cries, in a voice like a trumpet. "God!"— and falls downwards like a dead man on the grass.

He does not speak or move, not even when I go and kneel down by his side and entreat him to answer my voice, to make some sign.

"George, George!" I cry through my shuddering sobs; and then, for he may be dead, I say to myself in my wretchedness, I lay my hand upon the golden tressed head that lies so stirlessly on his folded arms.

"Do not touch me," he cries; "do not dare." . . .

Oh! the relief it is to me to hear his hoarse voice.

"I might have borne it yesterday; but not to-day—not to-day . . . the joy I have been hugging to my heart is all a myth —a sham. . . . I was putting myself in *his* place." . . .

A tremor shakes him; he buries his face deeper in his arms.

"In whose place?" I ask gently. "No one loves me but you, George!"

"No one but me?" he repeats, lifting his haggard face, all blotted and marred with grief and passion. "The man you love does not love you?"

"No," I say, subsiding into a tumbled, miserable heap by his side, while the tears trickle slowly down my pale cheeks. "You love me, George, and he loves somebody else, that is all!"

"Don't cry, darling," he says; "I can't bear it."

Even in this hour of supreme suffering my true, brave lover sets his own bitter grief aside to comfort mine.

"So that is the reason you look so pale

and thin? Nell, you are quite sure you love him?"

"Quite—quite sure, George!"

"It is not an idle fancy; you will hold to it?"

"Do you love me?" I ask. "Do you think that you will ever love any one else?"

"You know that I love you; and I am quite certain I shall never love any one else."

"Then, George," I say piteously, "as you feel for me, so I feel for him, and—— "

"I understand," he says; "I know." And a bitter heavy silence falls between us.

"And this man?" he says, waking out of it with a fiery anger that somehow comforts me. Who would not rather see a man swell with rage than bow his head in grief? "Who has worked this misery to you? Who has made you suffer like this? Who has dared?"

"It is not his fault," I say slowly; "it was all a mistake, George; all my own doing and vanity."

"I don't believe it," he cries, with flashing eyes. "*You* make love to any one? *you* let your heart go before it ever was asked for? Never! I have known you long enough, and well enough; and you could not have cared for this man without his having given you good reason."

"There was no reason," I say. "He told me he was in love with some one else. Could anything be plainer?"

"Did he tell you that at first—at the very beginning?"

"Not quite," I say, in a troubled voice; "but he did not know, he could not guess, that I should——"

A burning, shameful blush covers my cheeks, and dries up the salt pricking tears.

"By Heaven! he shall answer for it!" says George, between his teeth; and in his blue eyes is a fixed resolve that makes me tremble. "I will find him out, whoever or wherever he may be, and——"

"My poor fellow," I say, with a faint smile, "are you the one to seek redress for my imaginary wrongs? You are not my brother."

"For once I wish I were," he says

quietly; "I should. then have the right to punish the scoundrel who has dared to trifle with you. Nell, won't you tell me about it? We are not lovers now, you know—we are friends; and, dear, you need never fear my pestering you with unwelcome words and attentions: I thought no shame of entreating your love when there was a hope of my winning it; but now that I know how irrevocably it is given to another, and judging your heart by my own, I accept my fate and will bear it, please God, like a man. So could you not trust me, Nell?"

"I could trust you," I say very gently, for the tender pity of his voice almost breaks my heart; "but I cannot tell you, George. I have never spoken to any one living of it save you, and more than I have told you I shall never tell."

We have risen, and are now standing by the brook that leaps, and chatters, and froths, and fusses as it goes, pausing not a moment to look at the old old sight of a miserable man and girl who have wrecked their lives for love.

"Do not suppose that I do not care,"

I say passionately; " do not suppose that I do not *know*, George." . . .

" Yes, yes," he says ; " but you must not fret about me. Think of yourself, my poor little darling. If I could only bear it for you ! "

He breaks off, tries to speak again—fails ; then, without a word or sign, goes quickly away, and I stand still looking after him with aching, burning eyes, and the heaviest heart woman ever had. Have I passed the pure gold by to covet the baser metal? Could Paul Vasher ever love a woman as purely, as truly, and as unselfishly as George loves me ? There is a stronger, more selfish grit about Paul ; he will have his own way, and no one shall baulk him of it ; he will be master, and no one shall say him nay. He will assure his own happiness first, that of the woman he loves after ; and while George would look up to his idol, Paul would look down.

George is quite out of sight now, and with weary steps I go to the stile that divides the meadow from the field of rye and lean over it, thinking dully of that day

two months ago, when I made my wreath
and sent George away cross, and ran against
Paul Vasher in the midst of the ripe grain.

"History repeats itself," I say, half
aloud, as I watch those cunning workmen—
the ants, scurrying about at the base of the
primitive stone stile; "but only up to a
certain point, and there it always fails.
Now there is no Paul to come over the field
to-day; he is probably shooting with the
rest at Luttrell. I shall never have a
chance of seeing him here either, for after
to-day I will not come this way."

I lift my eyes, and see Paul Vasher coming across the field of rye to meet me. I
do not speak or stir; the hour has come,
and must be met; and somehow, perhaps it
is because my heart is so filled with George's
misery as to leave no room for pity of my
own, I feel a kind of indifference. "Nothing matters much now," I say to myself,
as Paul stands before me. He makes me
no greeting, nor do I him; he only looks
into my pale, tear-stained face with a quick
triumphant gladness that vaguely surprises
me. Why should he look so eager and

happy when his true love is nowhere near?

"I have come to claim the fulfilment of your promise," he says; then as I lift my eyes to his, he catches and holds them fast to his; and lo! my listlessness falls from me like a garment, and a living, writhing pain stirs and leaps in my dull heart, and I know that the old glamour is upon me, that all the world has faded away, and that in all my past, present, and future, naught has place save the dark beloved face that is looking so intently into mine.

"You never broke your word yet," he says, and his hands tightened their hold upon mine. "You will keep your promise, Nell."

With his eyes upon mine, with the resistless power he ever wielded over me compelling me, I open my lips to speak the truth as before my God; then I tear my hands out of his, my eyes from his.

"I cannot," I say with a bitter cry, "oh, I cannot!"

"Is it Paul?" he asks, folding his arms about me, and pressing my head down against his breast; "tell me, sweetheart."

" Tell me her name," I ask in a whisper;
" tell me quick."

" *Nell*, do you understand *now* ? "

As he lifts my arms and lays them about
his neck, as he bends his dark head and
seeks my lips with all the unsated hunger of
the first kiss, I turn my head quickly away
and hide it on his breast. Shall I receive
the kisses of this new lover while the
words uttered by the old one have scarcely
ceased to echo in my ears ?

" What is this ? " asks Paul, " holding
me away from him to look keenly into my
face: after all do you not love me, child?
I should have waited for an answer to my
question. Do you love me, my sweetheart,
my flower ? " he asks, looking into my face
with a passion of tenderness.

" Love you ? " I answer with a long, long
sigh. " What is love ? But let me go now,
Paul; let me go ! "

" Let you go ? " he says, smoothing my
hair back from my face, " now that I have
just got my little witch ? No ! I will keep
you safe enough, love, never fear ! "

" But you do not know," I say anxiously;

"you do not understand; it is so quick, so soon."

"Soon! and you have kept me at arm's length for more than a month! Ah! child, if you had known the restraint I had to put upon myself over and over again. I almost broke down."

"Did you love me all that time," I ask softly; "are you sure you did?"

"Loved you!" he says, "I think I have loved you ever since the Silverbridge days; I know I have loved you ever since the day I met you in yonder field. I never was so sorry to say good-bye to any one as when I said it to you under the porch at the Manor House, and all the while I was getting through that confounded business in town, I was fidgetting to get back to Silverbridge, and if it had not been for the absurdity of the thing, I should have come back just to get an hour's glimpse of you. Then I was obliged to go to the Luttrells, never dreaming they were relations of yours, and there I found you; and, sweet, I had not known you a week before I lost my head completely. Living as quietly as you did I never supposed for a moment that you could have had a lover; but very early in the day, from one or two chance remarks of yours, I gathered that you had; and never did a man chafe more under the knowledge than I. You would neither deny nor corroborate anything, and sometimes I felt certain you were beginning to care for me; sometimes, I believe, you were hankering after that man at Silverbridge, and at last——"

"You told stories," I say, laughing gently; "you told me you were in love with somebody."

"So I was."

"And that you would show her to me."

"So I will."

"And your behaviour was inexcusable."

"I know it; but why, you little minx, did you rout me so utterly that morning in the garden? I was telling you my love story full sail, on the point of asking you if you would try and love me, when out you tumbled a letter from your precious lover, with whom you told me, with inimitable *sang-froid*, you corresponded. And I had

fondly imagined (after getting over the first
unpleasant shock of your having a lover at
all), that you cared nothing about him,
flouted his attentions, and would none of
them! In self-defence I invented a fiction;
and even then, so stubborn you are, madam,
I could not gather from your face any more
than that you were disturbed, though
whether on his account or mine, I could
not for the life of me tell. I caught you
by a promise, child, and made up my mind
that here, where we first met, I would
ask you a plain question, receive a plain
answer."

"It is a plain answer," I say ruefully;
"for your sake I wish it were a prettier
one!"

"Little sweetheart!" he says, devouring
my face with his eyes, "do you remember
how I told you years and years ago to pray
that you might never grow up good-looking?
Well, I am glad you did not, for I could not
bear to lose a single one, not the very
smallest, of your charms—your lovely hair,
your sweet eyes, and sweeter lips. Nell,
what do you suppose I am made of?"

"Flesh and blood, I suppose," I answer, giving him a soft pinch.

"Well, then, I can't stand this; do you know that we have been here more than ten minutes, and that I have not had a single kiss; do you think I am so patient?"

"Not to-day, Paul," I say trembling, "some day perhaps, or to-morrow, but not to-day, I cannot because of—of him, you know."

"*Him?* there should be only one man in the world to you now, Nell."

"George Tempest," then I say, turning crimson; "*Lubin*, you know."

"What of him?" asks Paul in surprise; "surely you are not bothering your head about him? Poor devil! he must be cut up at losing a little pet like you; but it is not your fault, you can't help it. I have a notion "—he goes on, smoothing my cheek with his hand—" that this admirer of yours is a great, awkward, country-looking fellow, who does not know what to do with his arms and legs, in short, just what I first called him to you, a Lubin?"

"Perhaps you will see him some day," I

answer, smiling a little to myself at Paul's notion of George; it must be a source of small wonder, then, that I fell in love with himself. "Paul," I say gently, "do you know why I have been fretting to-day? do you know why I have been crying so bitterly?"

"Well," he says, looking down on me with a whimsical air of pride and amusement, "I thought that you might have been thinking a little bit about me, perhaps?"

"No, no," I answer, smiling rather sadly, "it was not of you I was thinking just then, but of Mr. Tempest, who had scarcely left me when you came; he was so wretched, and it seemed so soon, so indecently soon, for you to make love to me."

"And you care so much as that?" he asks, with a sudden jealousy in his voice that startles me; "you could be sorry for him; could think of him at such a time as this? Heaven knows I had no other woman in my thoughts when I told you that I loved you."

"Yes, I can," I answer steadily; "and I

should not be worthy of your love if I could fling away all memory of his great misery in one moment to lose myself in happiness with another lover the next."

"Did you ever care for that man?" he asks coldly, but he does not loose me out of his arms. "Did you ever have the smallest fancy for him?"

"Never!" I answer gravely; "if I had I should be with him, not you, at the present moment, should I not?"

He looks deeply into my eyes, and what he reads there must satisfy him, for he murmurs fond, mad love words over my drooped head, calls me his queen, his heart's delight, his idol.

"Papa may come this way," I say nervously; "he does not often, but he might; let us go and sit down in my parlour."

We cross the bare brown field, and reach my little green chamber, where a big log of wood affords us a seat, and sit down side by side.

"And now," he says, "I am going to show you my little girl;" and out of his breast-pocket he brings a velvet case, touches a spring, the lid flies back, and there, looking out at us from under a veil of hair and a wreath of poppies, is—me!

"How did you get it?" I ask, staring hard at it. (Surely, surely, I never was so pretty as that!)

"I asked an artist who was at the Luttrell's ball, to study your face and paint you with loose hair, and here it is."

(So it was my face that I left Paul to muse over that day on the terrace.)

"I have kissed this painted thing very often," he says, drawing me gently to his breast; "now the real lips are my own, do you deny them to me, Nell? I could take a hundred if I would, but I am too proud to do that; have you not one to give me, love?"

For a moment I tremble and hesitate; it is so soon, so terribly soon; if that other only knew! then, for my duty is to this my lord, I lift my lips to his, and as he folds me in his arms, he kisses me as I kiss him for the first time. Across that perfect kiss, than which the earth can give me no such other, why does a picture rise up before me, of a man and woman standing in the moonlight, wishing each other a passionate, last good-bye?

"If you were not so strong," I say, stroking his hand with my slim fingers, "I would keep you in such order, banish you to such a distance; you should sue so meekly for ever such a little favour!"

"If you were like that," he says, kissing me passionately on cheek and brow, and eyes and lips, (verily, one salute leads to a great many more!) "you would never have me at your feet. It is the soft, adorable, bewitching little creatures like you who get into a man's heart and stop there, though, Heaven knows! you kept me at a distance long enough!"

"I suffered for it enough!" I say, sighing. "Oh! I shall always consider you treated me very badly! It is a wonder my hair is not grey with all the misery I have had."

"My sweetheart!" he says.

Here there is a long and ridiculous pause, that people may fill up as they please.

"Do you know that I felt glad sometimes to see you looking sad? I thought you were fretting after Lubin; and I said to myself, 'Now she will know a little of what I am enduring.'"

Yes, he loves differently to George, not half as well; and I worship the very ground Paul walks on, and I esteem and like George as a brother.

It grows late, time has passed with such hurrying swiftness; through the dark stems of the trees before us shows the pale blue-green of the evening sky, cold and pure and beautiful exceedingly. Nature is robing herself in her cool twilight garment of silver grey, shrouding the trees and fields softly, as though preparing them for sleep; the sun has gone down, leaving a rack of amber and crimson clouds behind him; the leaves rustle gently in the autumn wind that wanders over the face of the land.

"I must go home now," I say, springing up. "But, Paul, Paul—*papa!*"

"What of him?" asks my lover, pinching my cheek.

"He is furious at the notion of any of his daughters thinking of such a thing as being married."

"And he married himself, and had twelve children," says Paul, "which points the moral. Well, I am going to call on him to-morrow, and I shall tell him that you and I——"

"Do not!" I say with much concern. "He would, first of all, kick you, or try to," I add, mentally measuring Paul's stalwart proportions; "then he would lock me up, and as he is going away in a fortnight for some months, it would be a serious business, for no one would dare to let me out."

"Poor little woman!" he says; "they shall not treat her like that while I am anywhere near!"

"If you would not mind waiting," I say wistfully; "if you would not say anything till he comes back, (it would not be very deceitful, would it?) we could have such a glorious time while he is away! I have been looking forward to such a dull one too," I add, thoughtfully; "but now I shall be able to get into *heaps* of mischief."

"And do you think I am going to wait for you all that time, child?" he asks;

"are you not afraid that my patience will wear out, and that I shall fall in love with somebody else?"

"No!" I answer saucily, "I am not in the least afraid! Will you wait, Paul?"

"He must not be away too long," says Paul, significantly, "or he won't find his daughter Nell waiting for him when he gets back. For your sake, though, what would I not do for your sweet sake? I will not speak to him about our marriage before he goes."

"Our marriage!" how sweet the words sound! As I muse on their goodness, like a chime of jingled silver bells sweep Silvia's words across my memory, "*You will never be Paul Vasher's wife, never!*"

Ay! but I am Paul Vasher's love, and that is what you are not, never will be, Silvia. Your wild words are very far away, very puerile and empty to me, as I stand with my lover's arms around me; harm can be worked between two lovers apart and misunderstanding each other, but what between two who are together in the first flush of acknowledged love and without a shadow between them?

We take a long while to make our adieux to our parlour and to cross the field, but now we are standing in the meadow arguing; *he* wants to see me safely in at the home gates, *I* want him to go back to The Towers, lest we meet any one. Where we now stand is perfectly retired, save in harvest-time or seed-time people rarely come this way, but the meadow once left, there is a chance of seeing anybody.

As we stand close together in the gloaming, talking our half-earnest, half-jesting nonsense, out of the gray shadow a man's figure emerges, and comes slowly towards us—George Tempest! He is looking down and walking heavily, with unstrung limbs and bent head; he does not see us until he almost brushes our garments, then he lifts his eyes, and, oh heavens! I could cry aloud at the dull misery of their regard—the set, fixed stupor of his face, with not a glint of hope or peace or every-day indifference in it—and my face is radiant with my new-found joy.

At first, although we are in his path, he does not seem to see us, and is about to pass on, when some gleam of consciousness comes across his face, his ordinary bearing comes back to him, his eyes brighten.

"George!" I say, stretching out my hand involuntarily; "George!"

He takes it as gently as though it were a flower.

"Is that you, Nell?" he asks in his natural voice; and then he looks at Paul, and, by some subtle intuition, *he knows:* I feel it in the sudden shock that passes from his hand to mine.

"You have not introduced me to your friend," he says.

Stumblingly I go through the form of introduction between the man I love and the man who loves me, then, I do not know how it comes to pass, we go on, and George passes on his way alone.

It is Paul who speaks first.

"And that is the man who loved you, Nell?" he says, slowly, "whom I have sneered at, pitied—I! Heavens, that I should dare! Sweetheart, are you sure that you love me—not him? He is noble, unselfish, grand, as I never was, never could be. It is not too late now; do you repent of the bad bargain you have made?"

"I love you," I answer, clasping my arms, of my own free will, about his neck; "I love you, my darling; what is any man in the world to me but a shadow, save you?"

"What is any woman on earth, what was one ever?" he asks, peering into my face through the closing darkness, "compared with what you are to me, my love, my idol, my wife?"

END OF VOL. II.

Caxton Printing Works, Beccles.

RECORD OF TREATMENT, EXTRACTION ETC.

Shelfmark: **12636 bb1**   **vol II**

S&P Ref No.   **74/42**

Microfilm No.

Date	Particulars	
	pH Before or Existing	pH After
12/99	**4.2**	**7.3**

Deacidification
Magnesium Bi Carbonate

Adhesives
wheat starch
animal glue

Lined / Laminated

Chemicals / Solvents

Cover Treatment

Other Remarks

Lightning Source UK Ltd.
Milton Keynes UK
UKOW021815130712

195954UK00007B/48/P